COMPELLING JOURNEY

Every life is a journey from the first moment of clarity to the last. Some keep our attention. This one has kept mine...Earl Stubbs

Anna Liza Herren Hampton

Grandmother

Earl Stubbs

Earl & Nancy Stubbs

Mike Stubbs  **Mark Stubbs**

Compelling Journey

PROLOGUE

This book was an itch that required scratching. The preparation gave me decades of entertainment and the opportunity to learn about my kin.

This record comes in four parts. The first is a family history of my paternal family, the Stubbs line. The second is a family history of my maternal ancestors, the Hampton line. Part III is a brief autobiography. Part IV is an anthology of autobiographical sketches written over a long period. Except for the first in the series, these stories are factual as I recall the incidents and are in chronological order.

I dedicate this book to my sons, Michael Wayne Stubbs (1957) and Mark Alan Stubbs (1960) both of whom I love and respect, and to my dear wife, Nancy Lynn Jacobs Stubbs for her proofreading, meaningful advice, and being the girl of my dreams.

All my love to my grandchildren: Travis, Jordan, Jennifer, Kayla, and Aaron. You bless my life.

Earl Stubbs-2012

Earl Stubbs

PART I

1

Life is full of surprises and serendipity--
Condoleeza Rice

THE STUBBS JOURNEY

The mystery man of the Stubbs clan is Joel Henry Stubbs born circa 1802 in the Spartanburg South Carolina, area. The unknown factor regarding Joel is that after fifteen years of trying, I am unable to establish the identity of his father with certainty. It is likely that he was Benjamin Stubbs of SC, but the evidence is not conclusive.

The SC Benjamin Stubbs fits most of the criteria of age, military record, etc. He enlisted after September 1, 1780, at the age of twenty. I assume he served until the end of the Revolutionary War in 1783. Then, he enlisted December 23-29, 1813, so he served in the War of 1812 as well. A substitute replaced him on April 30, 1816.

Compelling Journey

The census of 1800 shows Benjamin in the Union District of South Carolina with a male child that would fit Joel's age.

Joel surfaced in Spartanburg, SC, in the 1930 census. He was 28 at the time.

On 16 May 1846, Joel Henry Stubbs petitioned the congress, on behalf of his mother, for the Revolutionary War pension of his father, Benjamin Stubbs. The government "put aside" his request. This is a good indicator that Benjamin of South Carolina was Joel's father, but I am unable to establish Benjamin's lineage.

Joel's first foray into the field of matrimony was a marriage to Martha McMakin of South Carolina. She bore him six children, Sarah in 1831, Jane in 1833, Rebecca in 1835, Martha in 1838, Abbe in 1840, and Benjamin in 1842. The name of the boy child further supports the idea that Benjamin was Joel's father. The 1840 census shows Joel in Forsyth County, Georgia, with Martha McMakin Stubbs and five children.

Earl Stubbs

**Jane Stubbs
Daughter of Martha McMakin Stubbs
and
Joel Stubbs**

I accidently discovered this family when I inherited a box of old pictures. One of the pictures was of Jane Stubbs. Several of the photographs were of people named Pritchett. I traced the name and found that two of Joel's daughters, Martha and Rebecca, married a man named Benjamin Pritchett. He married Martha first, and when she died in 1871, he married Rebecca.

The Pritchett's moved from Newton County Georgia to Ft. Worth, Texas, and later had dealings with John Stubbs, one of Joel's sons. I must assume that the

Compelling Journey

Stubbs and Pritchett families kept in contact after the latter moved to Texas. (I connected with the Pritchett family in Ft. Worth and often correspond with Charles.)

2

**Familiarity breeds contempt and children.--
Mark Twain**

MARY ANN CAVENDER STUBBS

The 1850 census shows Mary Ann Cavender, age seventeen, living with Sarah and Dick Levie and working in a lint factory. Another unverified source indicates that Joel's future wife lived with her sister in Indian Springs, Georgia. Dick was 23 at the time and Sarah McIntosh was 21. Mary Ann was 17 and, likely, Sarah's sister.

Mary Ann was either Cherokee or Creek Indian. This was before the "Trail of Tears" when Andrew Jackson forced the Americanized Native Americans of the Southeast to Arkansas and then Oklahoma to reside in reservations.

At some point between 1840 and 1850, Martha McMakin Stubbs died. As was the pattern of the day, Joel needed help with his six children who ranged in age from seven to nineteen. He married Mary Ann Cavender on 2 July 1851.

Compelling Journey

I am not sure how Joel earned his livelihood, but one census shows him as a tin merchant. Another listed him as a carpenter.

Mary Ann was 18 years old when they married, and Joel was about 49. They produced their own family while caring for the remnants of Martha McMakin's. Josephine was their firstborn in January of 1853. Shortly after Josephine, Andrew Jackson arrived in October of 1853. Cynthia was born in 1856, and James came along six years later in 1859. Mary Ann bore John in 1864.

The family evolved when some of the older daughters moved out to marry and young ones arrived. Benjamin Prickett married Martha Stubbs in circa 1852. They had two children. Then, Martha passed. Rebecca, Martha's sister, lived with the Pricketts at the time. Benjamin married Rebecca, and they had a large family together. They migrated to Ft. Worth, Texas.

The 1860 census shows Rebecca and Benjamin with two children. Her sisters, Sarah, Jane, and Abbe, lived with the Pricketts.

Earl Stubbs

Mary Ann Cavender Stubbs
25 August 1833--1910

Whether or not Mary Ann was pure Native American or half is unknown, but during the 1950's, Native Americans from Oklahoma came to Flat Creek in Texas, and informed the Stubbs people that they were entitled to property on the reservation. Being suspicious by nature, the family members turned them away. I suspect that I am either 1/8 or 1/16 Native American. ES

When the war came, and the South lost many soldiers, the conscription rules became lax. In 1863, Joel at the age of sixty-one, served in the 64th Georgia Infantry for a period of one month. His enlistment was under the auspices of Captain Prickett.

Compelling Journey

Was this Benjamin Prickett or a relative of Benjamin's?

Joel furnished a man named Neil to substitute for him and became discharged on 14 April 1863 from Camp Cooper.

At this point, Joel disappeared from the records. I suspect that he died of natural causes sometime between 1863 and 1870, because the 1870 census shows Mary Ann Stubbs, listed as a widow and housekeeper, Cynthia, James, and John living in Butts County, Georgia. The same census lists James, age eleven, as farm labor.

*****

# 3

You can't have a light without a dark to stick it in.--Arlo Guthrie

THE MIGRATION TO TEXAS

My ancestors on my father's side came from Georgia. As did so many families of the nineteenth century, worn out farms drove them west.

While sitting in a corner listening to my two elderly aunts, Valary and Ella Clyde, reminisce about the adventures of their family members, I often heard references to Aunt Jo and Aunt Cynthia or "Cynthy," as they called her. Since both of their families migrated to Flat Creek in about 1890 along with other members of our family, my aunts spoke of them on several occasions.

Aunt Josephine married William "Bill" Floyd and produced eight children. The names Annie, Charlie, Willie, Alice, and Effie are familiar to me from conversations of the older people. Willie was a woman named for her father. That was a common practice. She was a handsome woman who never married. My mother's

Compelling Journey

name is Willie Gertrude, named for her father William Henry Hampton as well.

Pictures of Cynthia show that she was a great beauty. She married Noah Parker who became a notorious murderer. They produced four children, Aube, Thomas, Alice, and William "Bill." When her family migrated to Texas, Cynthia took her children and left Noah in prison in Georgia where he died.

Tom Parker, Cynthia and Noah's son, was a close friend and cousin of my family, the Prices. He was quite elderly when I knew him, and he lived with the Morelands outside of Naples, Texas. They were relatives of his deceased wife, Molly. As fate would have it, Coy Moreland was my classmate through twelve years of public school. Tom spent a great deal of time visiting in our home. I recall that he had a hole in his chin left from removing a cancer.

The rolling, sandy hills of Northeast Texas duplicated the terrain around Covington, Georgia. The immigrants transplanted many of the names from Georgia to their new home. Flat Creek, DeKalb County, Douglasville, and Marietta near Atlanta, Georgia are examples.

Earl Stubbs

John Thomas Stubbs
15 January 1864--29 May 1929

Due to a sawmill accident, John had only one arm. Both he and my grandfather, Jim, were volatile men. After the migration to Texas, they argued and John fired his shotgun at Jim who stepped behind a tree. Fearing Jim's retribution, John took his family and headed for Ft. Worth where he contacted Benjamin F. Prickett, the husband of his half-sister, Martha.

John was a shrewd businessman. He bought a herd of cattle in Ft. Worth, drove them back to Georgia, and started a cattle ranch. Then, according to his progeny, John accumulated a million dollars mostly through land speculation and the sale of cattle. However, a bank

Compelling Journey

failure robbed him of his financial gains, but according to family lore, he recouped his million before he died.

James Madison Stubbs
23 March 1859—20 April 1944

    Since Jim and John had endured so many hardships together as children, their estrangement couldn't last. Eventually, they corresponded by mail leading to a visit to Flat Creek by John to mend the fences.
    During the 1980's, when I managed the Southeastern USA for Fisons Limited, I visited Covington, Georgia, seeking out relatives. The first place I searched was the courthouse. It didn't take long to discover that the county clerk's name was Tom Stubbs. A visit with him

Earl Stubbs

established that he was John's grandson, the son of Lester for whom my father was named.

Eventually, I found Johnny Caswell Johnson, John's great grandson. We collaborated on the present Stubbs/Johnson family tree, visited on two occasions, and became life-long friends. He is another distant relative I email most days.

Compelling Journey

Lucy Delula Ivey Stubbs
18 April 1860—15 March 1933

Before the family migrated to Texas, Jim Stubbs lived near the James W. Ivey family and his wife Arenna, Arena, or Irena. Jim married Lucy, one of their daughters, so James and Arenna are my great-grandparents. James Ivey was sixty-six when Jim and Lucy relocated to Texas.

Valary was Jim and Lucy's firstborn. She arrived in 1878 in Georgia. She was about eleven years old when the resettlement to Texas occurred. She loved her grandparents and the separation from them was difficult.

Flat Creek Missionary Baptist Church
Established 1868

Members of the Flatcreek Community established this church in 1868, many years before the Stubbs family arrived. While it is not active at this time, interested parties meet here once each year to conduct cemetery business, sing traditional hymns, and share a meal much in the same way as has occurred for the past 145 years.

Compelling Journey

Most of the older generations of Stubbs lie in the cemetery, including my parents, grandparents, aunts, and uncles, and cousins. A permanent endowment supports both the cemetery and church. Visiting this relic provides a warm feeling in my heart knowing how many loved ones graced its pews and raised their voices in worship.

My father, Marvin Stubbs led the singing for years. The church deacons turned out my guardian, Ella Clyde Stubbs Price, for dancing. She, of all people, could have used the influence. No Christian saint more deserved the title than my Aunt Augusta Stubbs due to her unfailing worship and worldly deeds.

4

**Man is born to live, not to prepare for life--
Boris Pasternak**

JIM'S FAMILY

Valary Stubbs, Jim and Lucy's firstborn child, married Benjamin Weatherby Taylor in 1899. They produced six children, five of which lived until adulthood. They were Stella Glyn in 1903, Mattie Inez in 1905, James Curtis in 1908, Era Aline in 1910, Benjamin Weatherby Jr. in 1917, and Royce Allen in 1921. James Curtis died young.

Stella Glyn Taylor Camp was always one of my favorites. When Uncle Ben retired from the farm, they moved to a house in Mt. Pleasant just behind Stella Glyn and her family. She married Cullen Camp. Their firstborn was Marie. Bill came next and served in World War II in the USN. He was a tragic figure who suffered from emotional problems and emphysema in later life. Bobby Joe Camp was a good high school football player and a smart guy. He educated himself and had a successful life

Compelling Journey

as a banker. Glen Dale, the youngest, owned a one truck moving business when I last saw him in 1970.

My Aunt, Valary Stubbs Taylor, wrote the following account. I spent many hours as a youngster listening to her, Tom Parker, and Ella Clyde tell this story. The Mt. Pleasant paper published it before her death in 1969--ES

The Journey to Texas
By Valary Delula Stubbs Taylor

My maiden name was Valary Delula Stubbs. I was born in Atlanta, Georgia, in 1879. My favorite book has always been and will always be the Bible. I would be glad to hear from any of my relatives that knew me in Georgia.

As my mind drifts back to the days of my childhood, it seems only yesterday that my younger brother Walter and I worked in the cotton mill in Atlanta, Georgia, when we weren't in school. I was twelve and Walter was nine-years-old. The work in the factory was very hard, as they didn't have the modern methods of spinning thread they have now. I worked at the spinning frame where the thread wound on the bobbin. Walter drove a little car over the factory picking up the full bobbins of thread.

When we weren't working, Walter and I walked three miles to school. It was called Hope School located near Covington, Georgia. I shall never forget our teacher, Miss Era Allen. (My Aunt Valary named two of her children for

Earl Stubbs

her teacher. She named a daughter Era and a son Royce Allen…ES)

After two months of working at the cotton mill, Pa decided we would move back to the country near Covington, Georgia. It was not far from Stone Mountain and the Alcova River. Ella was little and that's where Carl was born.

My favorite place to visit was the home of Grandpa and Grandma Ivy. Her maiden name was Rena Morris and Grandpa's name was Jim. They lived in a large house made of logs with several apartments. Grandma's kitchen was separated from the rest of the house. It had a large iron stove and a fireplace for preparing food. I thought no one could cook like Grandma Ivy.

Grandpa was a good man. He would always go on his friends note to borrow money, and lots of times, they would not pay him back, but Grandpa seemed to enjoy helping others.

I didn't know my grandparents on my dad's side very well. My Grandpa Stubbs had yellow red hair and was from Europe. It is said that he came from Germany and had the true German accent. (Born in South Carolina in 1802, it is not likely that Joel would have a German accent. His father was a Revolutionary War Veteran and could have emigrated with the Hessians from Germany. Joel could have grown up in a German-speaking family. The 1870 census shows Valary's grandmother, Mary Anne Stubbs as a widow, with her 11-year-old son, Jim

Compelling Journey

Stubbs, working as farm labor. Obviously, Valary's information came from her father and grandmother...ES)

Grandma Stubbs was a full blood Cherokee Indian. (At this time, I am unable to find my great grandmother in the Cherokee rolls. The Creek tribe was numerous in the area, so she is likely Creek. I cannot prove if she was a full blood Native American or half. If her pictures are accurate, she appears full blood. Some reports show her as the daughter of Sarah McIntosh, the daughter of a wealthy Native American of the time, but these claims are unsubstantiated and unreliable...ES) *Her maiden name was Mary Anne Cavendar. She was a pretty woman with long black hair and dark eyes. She was also a very brave woman.*

Once while Grandpa Stubbs fought in the Civil War Grandma and her children sat by the fireside. She smoked her clay pipe and had a gun nearby for protection. She heard a knock at the door. It was Yankee soldiers.

They forced their way into the house. They had already stolen the cured ham and other food from the smoke house. They had stolen the horses from Grandma's lot. One of the Yankee soldiers walked to the fireplace, lit his pipe, and then he asked Grandma where she had the rest of her horses hidden.

When she told him that was all we had, they said, "Ah, you are lying."

Finally, they left with whatever loot they already had. I heard many stories like this that are true. There were the

Earl Stubbs

burned buildings and factories, and I was told that Yankee soldiers did this, but I was too young to know that war leaves scars like this.

A lot of times we children would play by the Alcova River, wade in the edge of the water, and walk on the big, flat rocks. We didn't realize the danger of playing near the river. It was very deep in some places. One day while we were walking on the rocks my brother Carl fell off, and I had to drag him out.

After living in Georgia for some time, Pa decided we should move to Texas. There were about a dozen of us to make the trip. Uncle Pie (John) Stubbs and his family had already moved Texas. There was Ma and her children and Aunt Cynthia Parker and her children to make the trip. Pa had come to Texas ahead of us to find a place to live.

I will never forget how sad I felt having to leave Grandma and Grandpa Ivy. We spent our last night in Georgia at their house. The next day they went with us to the train and watched us until we were out of sight.

The train drove upon a large ferryboat and it took us to the other side of the river where we began our journey to Texas. The trip was very tiring as the trains traveled slowly in those days. They had not been in use very long.

Aunt Cynthia's children's names were Tom, Alice, Aube, and Bill Parker. Tom was the oldest; he was seventeen and he brought his gun along to protect us. There was Ella, Carl, Walter, Ma, and me.

Compelling Journey

Our destination was Jefferson, Texas, with its beautiful cypress trees and open saloons. This was where we spent our first night.

Two suspicious men approached us at the train station, and we asked them where we could get a hotel room for the night. They directed us to one, but after we had registered and got to our room, we decided the place was rough, so Ma, Aunt Cynthia, and Tom with his gun nearby sat up all night. The rest of us went to sleep.

About nine o'clock that night the suspicious looking men came to our hotel room and knocked on the door.

"What do you want?" asked Tom.

"Oh, we just came to tell you your train is here."

We knew better as our train wasn't due until 7 a.m. the next morning. Tom told the men we would wait until 7 a.m. to leave. Finally, the men left.

The next morning our train was on time, and a while later, we arrived in Hughes Springs, Texas, where Pa and Uncle Pie Stubbs met us.

We spent the next night at Uncle Pie's (John) house, and the next day we moved to a farm Pa had rented for us from Mr. Henry Allen.

*****

Earl Stubbs

Valary Delula Stubbs Taylor
&
Benjamin Weatherby Taylor

Mattie Inez, Valary's second child, was a Bohemian type who enjoyed writing poetry and singing with her brother Royce. She adopted a child named Ben Marlin Nix.

The next child, Era, was a beautiful woman who never married. There was talk of a broken heart when young. B. W. survived the worst of World War II and still lives in Commerce, Texas, in 2012, but his health is frail. He is ninety-four, and spent his life as a carpenter. I

Compelling Journey

wrote his military memoir and visit him often. The army changed his name from B. W. to Benjamin Weatherby, which was his father's name. He made it permanent.

Royce was a musician and songwriter. He played the piano and sang from memory what appeared to be a limitless storehouse of songs. As a child, I sang with Royce when the opportunity presented itself. Once, at the peak of his career, when he played at the Adolphus Hotel's Century Room in Dallas, he invited me to perform with him, but I could never bring myself to do it. I just knew I would forget the words to the songs, and I probably would have.

After her passing, Aunt Valary's family buried her at Bradfield's Chapel Cemetery near Daingerfield, Texas, on the day that the number one ranked Texas Longhorns, and the number two Arkansas Razorbacks played for the national title in 1970. I listened to this classic football game while driving home from her funeral.

*****

Next came Walter James in 1881. Born in Georgia as well, Uncle Walter was unusual in that he was a robust, athletic man. According to family lore, he was a baseball player of major league quality. That is likely true, since one of his progeny, Rick Stubbs, became a world-class hurdler, and Rick's son, Drew, played centerfield for the Cincinnati Reds.

Earl Stubbs

Walter lost two fingers due to an accident at a sawmill in Texas. Such injuries were common.

**Walter and Augusta Stubbs and two
Children Lois Faye and Bernice Hershel**

Walter married a great beauty, Augusta Mauldin. She was a favorite of all who knew her. Their marriage produced ten children including Bernice Herschel in 1901, Lois Faye in 1903, Lula Adelle in 1907, Joseph Weldon in 1909, Dorothy Mozelle 1912, Mona Rae and W. J. (Twins) in 1915, Thera Maxine in 1918, David Quincy in 1920, and Francis Laverne in 1922. I knew them all.

Compelling Journey

Herschel was a throwback in that he was a tall man ... the first in the Stubbs line. He and my father Marvin were contemporaries, and Marvin described him as a good baseball player. He was the grandfather of Rick Stubbs, and the great-grandfather of Drew Stubbs.

Lois never married. She had friends in Mineral Wells and lived there off and on. Mostly, she lived at home in Flat Creek with her parents. She suffered from lifelong allergies.

Lula died at the age of three.

Weldon became a country storeowner and fell to an assassin's bullet in Queen City, Texas, in 1968. His killer escaped detection.

Mozelle married Billy Barnwell and produced two children.

Mona married Reffer Bradford and produced six children.

W. J. married late in life and sired no children. He served his country during World War II as a flight instructor. Following the war, he achieved financial success as a homebuilder near Mt. Pleasant, Texas.

Maxine was a striking, red-haired woman. She married Ocie Riggins, and they produced three children. She died of cancer at a young age.

David survived World War II, but never adjusted to life before or after the war. According to a contemporary of his, our grandfather, Jim, gave him home brew on a regular basis while David was in the first grade.

Earl Stubbs

Apparently, he had a significant problem with alcohol, since he died in a car wreck, not long after World War II, while under the influence.

Laverne was a handsome woman as well. She married Weldon Wommack, and they produced two children. At this writing, she remains alive at the age of ninety.

*****

Ella Clyde Stubbs was the third child of Jim and Lucy's born in Georgia. She married Judson Dudley Price, and they had two children one of which died after only a few days. Ella Clyde never got over the loss of this boy-child, and a hysterectomy due to cervical cancer. Both scarred her permanently and turned her into a bitter woman.

Their daughter, Ella Mae Price, married John L. Barker in 1927, produced no children, and their union ended in divorce in 1940.

Ella Clyde was a temperamental, unhappy woman who had difficulty with personal relations. She had the capacity to turn on the charm and entertain at will, but she was suspicious and mean-spirited by nature. She dominated my life until I learned the rules of the game and could wear her down with unceasing pressure. I confess to being the one person on the planet whom she loved. I suspect it was because I stood up to her.

Compelling Journey

Ella Clyde Stubbs Price
7 July 1883—25 January 1972

The next child born to Lucy and Jim in 1886 did not make the trip to Texas. John Robert lived six months.

Carl arrived in 1889 in Newton County, Georgia. He married Ada Carurle. He was a markedly handsome man. Ada was a beauty as well. It was only natural that they produced a bevy of gorgeous daughters. They were Christine in 1910, Lillian in 1912, Jewell in 1915, Margare in 1917, Madison in 1920, and Jacqualine in 1926. Madison, the only son, died at the age of two.

Lillian married Oneal Lee, and they had three children. One of them, Doyce Lee, and I served on the board of the Texas A&M-Commerce Alumni Association until his unexpected death from a heart attack. He was a

Earl Stubbs

former Texas State Representative, attorney, and Texas State Insurance Commissioner.

Carlton S. Stubbs
1 October 1889—17 May 1966

Born in Texas, Liller came next in 1891. She lived seven years and lies in the Flat Creek Cemetery.

Altha Mary was born in 1894 and passed in 1902. She lies in the Flat Creek Cemetery.

Edgar came next in 1897. A tragic figure, Ed suffered from epilepsy and dementia. He died in 1939. I attended his funeral. It is the first that I can recall.

Marvin Lester, our father, was the last child. He arrived in 1900. He was more studious than his siblings were, so he attended the Flat Creek School through the eighth grade. That was a significant education during those times.

Marvin, though small in stature, was a good baseball player in his own right. He was a curveball pitcher, but lack of knowledge about how to condition or care for his pitching arm caused him to injure tendons and ligaments to the extent that he was no longer effective. He said that he threw his arm away.

Marvin is at the top right. His cousin, Hershel, is the tall boy in the back. The first boy on the bottom row on the left is J. O. Jordan. Next to him is Hershel's brother, Weldon. Their sister, Lois, is in the middle of the third row standing by the boy with the white shirt.

Earl Stubbs

GERTRUDE & MARVIN STUBBS

EARL STUBBS  **NANCY STUBBS**

5

Citizens are not born but made--Spinoza

THE FLAT CREEK COMMUNITY

I was born in 1902 in a log cabin with mortar made out of post oak clay and lime to stop cracks. I guess they did not have cement in those days. In 1905, my dad built a rough boxing plank house and rented the log cabin to other people.

That was about twenty years after Flat Creek Community, church, and the schoolhouse was built. (The members built the church in 1868. I suspect the community came before that...ES) *There was some cleared land, but most was in woods. There were acres of timber in pine trees. They said that these trees were two hundred years old. Some were five feet thick.*

Indians had roamed over those woods. My daddy said they had deer and wild turkey. Clark and Boyce Lumber Company, at Jefferson, Texas, bought the timber and built a railroad track up to Marietta, Texas. They called it TNW railroad, and it came through Flat Creek Community. They

Earl Stubbs

used oxen and slips to fill up and dig in the ground as much as twenty feet deep at places to lay the railroad track. They got the train running, cut the timber, and hauled it by train to Jefferson to have it cut into lumber. Most of the lumber was #1 grade with no knots in it. Then the ground where the timber had stood was cleared up and made into farmland.

Back to the church. In time, when I was about twelve years of age, a lot of people went to that church. Some folks went horseback and some in wagons. There was not much money to pay the preacher. Some congregations paid money. Others paid with syrup, corn, and produce. There was not any price promised to pay the preacher.

Around the first of July, we held a big revival meeting. It was for a week, day and night. Not all could get in the house. I remember when the girls had a boyfriend; they would go in the church together. She would have a folding fan. She would fan her boyfriend and herself in the hot weather. So many went to church, especially at night, they went to building brush arbors to have service. In and around the arbor for light at night, they would get jugs of kerosene (it only cost ten cents a gallon); put ropes in the mouth of the jugs for a wick, and hang them up around the arbor for light. If you sat close to the light, you would have to knock bugs out of your face.

Some of the ancestors of the old time settlers back in the eighteenth century might remember some of these names. Dr. McMichael, (Jim and Griff McMichael's father)

Compelling Journey

B. L. Brooks, Jim Stubbs, Uncle Blue Maulden, Cliff Welch, Mr. Wynnigar, Tab Meggs, Will Tindol, Albert Jordan, Elbage Duncan, Mr. Sam Adams, W. C. Jordan, Jimmy Jordan, R; L. Jordan, Dick Barton. Mr. Bill Floyd. Others were Hollis Davenport, Sim Arnold, Will Arnold, Emma Campbell, Mr. Buck Knight, Mrs. Sallie Thomas, Mrs. Can Irvin, Albert C. Jordan, Edgar Westbrook, and Mr. Boney. Most of the above generations came from Alabama and Georgia and settled in Flat Creek Community. Most all of them had children that grew up and had children that caused a large number of people to live in that community, but about all of them have moved away now.

Now back to the school. We had only one room and one teacher for all grades. At that time, they had school five months a year and paid the teacher $35 to $45 a month. The teachers would whip the ones going to school with long switches when they misbehaved. We drank water from a spring from one dipper. The moss would get stirred up in the spring, and we would drink moss with the water. The spring was about four hundred yards from the schoolhouse. All along there would be a fight at the spring, but we would not tell the teacher. A pine thicket was across the road from the schoolhouse. We used it for our toilet.

When Hannah and I moved back from Amarillo, Texas, in 1928, we settled in Flat Creek Community. There were a lot of people living in that area. We liked the folks and decided to settle with them. We tried several things to

Earl Stubbs

make a living. We bought some farming land including bottomland, but then decided to put in a general mercantile business. We handled everything that people wanted, including furniture.

We added the milk goat business, so I had all of our land fenced goat proof. I sent two men in a large truck to Arkansas to buy a truckload of milk goats. They brought back fifty goats and put them in the pasture with some cows and geese. In about five months, the goats started dying. I decided to dehorn them, so we did. Behold! All of them had worms eating into their heads from inside of their horns. I got my shotgun and killed them all. So I failed in the goat business. We didn't know what else to try, so we thought it over for a few months and decided to having and raising some children. With the community's help, we raised three sons. (I attended East Texas State with Jimmy...ES)

Folks, especially those living back in the country, did not go to a hospital. As long as we could get Dr. Jenkins, we thought we were safe, and we were. Hannah was pregnant with one of the boys and the time was getting close. We had a big snow, and it rained on top of the snow. The rain froze on top of the snow. People could hardly make it over the roads. One of the elderly women, yes I remember it was Mrs. Hattie Davenport, she loved us a lot. She telephoned Hannah and told her to hold that baby back until the road got better so Dr. Jenkins could

Compelling Journey

get over it. We just laughed and thought everything would be okay, and it was.

Another time, the roads were in the same shape. A fellow came to the store out of breath, scared in a tremble, and wanted me to telephone Dr. Hibbith at the hospital to come to his house. His wife was having trouble trying not to have a baby because of the bad roads. I phoned the doctor to come. He wanted to know what the trouble was. I told him they were having family trouble. He said, "They don't need me, they need the sheriff." I told him it was not that kind of trouble. It was trouble that they need a doctor. "You mean having a baby?" He said.

I said, "Yes." I was too timid to tell him the real trouble.

He said he could not get over the roads; someone would have to come after him. I said I would send someone to get him. I put chains on the car wheels and sent after him. Everything worked out okay.

At that time, we did not have electricity in the Flat Creek Community. We used wash pots and tubs to wash in. After our kids were born, we had more washing to do. I had a good washhouse. I found a May tag washing machine in Dallas that had a gasoline motor to run the machine. Hannah had a black lady wash for her. It was about twelve feet from the washtubs to the washing machine. While the motor was running, she thought she had to go at a run from the washing machine to the tubs, because the motor was running.

Earl Stubbs

They were buying refrigerators in Dallas and selling iceboxes. I went to Dallas, bought the iceboxes, brought them back, and sold them. Since I sold a lot of iceboxes, I thought I would build a large icehouse and sell ice. I did not think to ask someone that knew how to build an icehouse for advice. So I got a lot of sand and cement and built a concrete icehouse. I got a big load of ice and put it in the icehouse one hot morning. The next morning I went out to see about the ice. I opened the door, and I did not have any ice. It had all melted. So it turned out like the milk goat business - I gave up.

While I was in the store business in Flat Creek Community, a young man dated an elderly man's daughter. The couple wanted to get married. Mr. Elderly Man did not want that to happen. So the girl jumped out of the window one night, and they got married. That made Mr. Elderly Man mad. He got his shotgun, came to the store, and asked for some shells that had buck shot in them. I said that I did not have any buck shot shells, but had some with #4 shot shells. He said, "Maybe that will get him." I asked him was he going to try to kill a deer.

He said, "I am going to kill a son of you know what." Some time the next day, the young man came to the store with his gun and asked for the same kind of gun shells. He heard about her daddy carrying a gun to kill him.

For about two weeks one would bob up at the store, and in a day or two, the other would bob up at the store. Both would have their gun across their shoulder. After

Compelling Journey

about two weeks, they stopped carrying their guns. I was uneasy that they might meet at the store and have a shoot-out.

One Christmas, we had a turkey shooting at the store. There was a large crowd. They got through with the turkey shooting and several came in the store. Of course, some were drinking. We were waiting on customers. One of the men came up to me and told me about a man that was drinking and had stolen some merchandise from me and put them in his wagon. I went to the door, asked him did he get some goods that he forgot to pay for. He came back in the store with his long blade knife open, waving his knife close to my stomach, cursing me. I stood still, not saying a word. When he got through cursing me, he went back to the wagon and went home. Early the next morning, he brought the groceries back and said the reason he acted like he did was because he was drinking. He wanted me to forgive him. I said to him that I would. So that was the end of that.

We had a customer come to the store. He was a black man, and he owed me about $35.00. He sold some timber and had some money. Every time he got a hundred or two dollars in his pocket, he would go crazy and come to the store. I was in an offset room cutting hair. I went to a barber school before I married, and I cut hair in connection with the store. My oldest brother was working in the store with me. This black man walked up to the counter showing his money. In a joking way, I asked him what

Earl Stubbs

about loaning me some of that money. He said, "Okay, how much do you want?"

I said, "About $25.00." He loaned me $25.00. It came in my mind that I would give him credit for it in the book. That was what I did, but he did not know about that.

Two or three days after that, he came back to my house at about three o'clock in the morning and wanted in the store. Well, crazy me got up and let him in my store. I turned the light on. He rolled up his sleeves, drew his arms up to show his muscle. They looked large to me. He brought his right arm down toward my face. His mind was way off since he did not talk with any sense at all. He went to mumbling. I could not understand what he was saying. Finally, he made me understand that he wanted me to take him to Linden. He was foaming at the mouth by then. I told him to get hold of himself. I could not carry him because I had to stay with my family.

I had to try some way to get him out of the store. So I told him to go over to my brother's house, he might take him to Linden. In that way, I got him out. I was about crazy as he was by that time and scared. He started over to my brother's house. I ran in, got Hannah and the kids up, told her and the kids to go to my mother's house, so they did. I was sure that crazy man would come back.

Our telephones were out of shape. I had a little house out from my house. There was a man helping me. I waked him up and asked him to go quickly to another neighbor's house and call the sheriff to come out there as soon as

Compelling Journey

possible. We had a crazy man that was dangerous. He jumped up, scared to death. He was shaking so bad, I was afraid he would wreck the car. I went on to my mother's house. From her house, we could see the store. That crazy man did come back, but there was not anyone anywhere about the store but him. He left again. The law came, got him, and sent him off to the asylum. In a day, maybe two, one of his sons came to the store. I told him how things were and showed him the account that his dad had with me, about the $25.00. I gave him credit on the account. He paid me the difference and that was all over and was I glad.

I think this is enough to tell about Flat Creek Community at one time. I love Flat Creek people and also love other people.

*****

According to my father, Marvin Lester Stubbs, J. O. Jordan was his best friend. Their connections intertwined for the majority of their lives. They went to the Flat Creek School together. J. O.'s store was within easy walking distance from Marvin's house. J. O. married Hannah. Marvin married my mother, Gertrude Stubbs, who passed at the age of thirty-one. After twenty years alone, Marvin married Bonnie McKinney who was Hanna's sister...ES

Earl Stubbs

Marvin loved to sing. He was a natural tenor, and attended several itinerant music schools studying shaped notes as opposed to round notes. He led the singing at the Flat Creek Church for many years. He served as road commissioner as well. He enjoyed a certain amount of popularity and respect in Flat Creek that he never established elsewhere.

Marvin, Ed, Valary, Jim, Carl, & Ella 1939

Compelling Journey

Marvin married Willie Gertrude Hampton, known as "Gerti" to her family members. She and Marvin produced three children: Anna Marvalynn in 1925, Dorothy Jean in 1930, and Earl Wayne, your tried and true reporter, in 1934.

Lynn married Blewett Cotton and spent most of her life in New Mexico. They produced two children, Carol and Gary. After Blewett's untimely death in a private plane crash, she, successfully, ran their company, Cotton Butane, for the better part of thirty years.

I was Dot's student during her first year as a teacher. She married Joe Tom Terrell, and they had one son, Tommy Jack.

I am the youngest child of the youngest child of the James Madison Stubbs line. I married Nancy Lynn Jacobs of Farmersville, and we have two sons, Michael Wayne born in 1957 and Mark Alan born in 1960. Our five grandchildren are Travis-1987, Jordan-1990, Jennifer-1995, Kayla-1995, (Twins), and Aaron-1996.

*****

6

I compiled the following family tree in conjunction with Johnny Johnson, a relative from the progeny of John Stubbs, brother to James Madison Stubbs. Johnny compiled the Georgia Stubbs family branch. This version includes only the James Madison's family and is far from complete.

STUBBS FAMILY TREE

..... 1 Joel Henry Stubbs (1802 - 1864) b: 1802 in Spartanburg, Spartanburg, South Carolina, USA, d: 1864 in Georgia, USA

..... + Martha McMakin (1812 - 1849) b: Abt. 1812 in South Carolina, USA, m: Abt. 1829 in Newton, Georgia, United States, d: Abt. 1849 in Newton County, Georgia, USA

.... 2 Sarah Ann Stubbs (1831 -) b: 1831 in South Carolina, USA

.... 2 Jane Stubbs (1833 -) b: 1833 in South Carolina, USA

.... 2 Rebecca Ann Stubbs (1835 - 1871) b: 22 Mar 1835 in South Carolina, USA, d: 23 Nov 1871 in Douglas, Georgia, United States

.... + L. W. Pritchett (1828 - 1910) b: Jan 1828 in South Carolina, USA, d: 01 Feb 1910 in Wood, Texas, USA

.... 2 Martha Elizabeth Stubbs (1838 - 1891) b: Abt. 1838 in Spartanburg, South Carolina, d: 07 Nov 1891 in Tarrant County,

Compelling Journey

Texas

.... 2 Abbe Stubbs (1841 -) b: 1841 in Georgia, USA
.... 2 Benjamin Stubbs (1843 -) b: 1843 in Georgia, USA
...... + Mary Ann Cavender (1833 - 1910) b: 25 Aug 1833, m: 13 Feb 1851 in Newton, Georgia, USA, d: Abt. 1910 in Cass, Texas, USA
.... 2 Josephine Francis Stubbs (1852 - 1933) b: 01 Jan 1852 in De Kalb, Georgia, USA, d: 04 Apr 1933 in Cass, Texas, USA
.... + William Franklin Floyd (1851 - 1938) b: 18 Dec 1851 in Georgia, USA, m: 1872, d: 12 Dec 1938 in Cass, Texas, USA
.... 3 Annie Floyd (1873 -) b: 25 Nov 1873 in Jasper, Georgia, USA
.... + Fnu Copeland
.... + Benjamine Brooks
.... 3 James Charles Floyd (1876 - 1944) b: 02 Jun 1876 in Georgia, USA, d: 05 Apr 1944 in Hughes Springs, Cass, Texas, USA
.... + Ada Louisa Maulden (1880 - 1962) b: 11 May 1880, m: 25 Mar 1900 in Cass, Texas, USA, d: 27 May 1962
.... 4 Ethel Floyd (1901 - 1975) b: 08 Jan 1901 in Cass, Texas, USA, d: 03 Mar 1975 in Springdale, Benton, Arkansas, USA
.... + Tom Poplin m: 14 Oct 1919
.... 4 Lula Floyd (1903 - 1989) b: 11 Feb 1903 in Cass, Texas, USA, d: 19 Dec 1989 in Harris, Texas, USA
.... + W J Blanton m: 22 Mar 1919
.... 4 Alley Lee Floyd (1905 - 1982) b: 17 Sep 1905 in Cass, Texas, USA, d: 14 Dec 1982 in Fayette, Calhoun, Arkansas, USA

Earl Stubbs

.... + Glenn Hayes m: 19 Oct 1919

.... 4 Mary Floyd (1907 - 1920) b: 21 Nov 1907 in Cass, Texas, USA, d: 26 Sep 1920 in Texas, USA

.... 4 Willie Dennis Floyd (1910 - 1985) b: 02 Jun 1910 in Cass, Texas, USA, d: 16 Feb 1985 in Cass, Texas, USA

.... + Exar I. Shaddix (1911 - 1989) b: 06 Mar 1911 in Cass, Texas, USA, m: 23 Sep 1928 in Morris, Texas, USA, d: 09 Dec 1989 in Linden, Cass, Texas, USA

.... 5   Dorthy Lee Floyd (1929 -) b: 19 Aug 1929 in Cass, Texas, USA

.... + Tony Calvin Reese m: 28 Jul 1947 in Texas, USA

.... 5   Louis Doil Floyd (1931 -) b: 29 May 1931 in Cass, Texas, USA

.... + Martha A. Parker m: 11 Aug 1956 in Texarkana, Bowie, Texas, USA

.... 5   Delta Reece Floyd (1934 -) b: 05 Nov 1934 in Cass, Texas, USA

.... + Jack Afton Jones m: 16 Feb 1958 in Texas, USA

.... 6 Sue Marcel Jones (1958 -) b: 17 Nov 1958

.... + Charles Kenneth Ballew m: 15 Apr 1953 in DALLAS TX.

.... 6 Charlott Marsha Ballew (1954 -) b: 04 Jan 1954 in DALLAS TX.

.... + Silas Edward Hamilton m: 05 Apr 1960 in Bay City, Matagorda, Texas, USA

.... 6 Minnie Reina Hamilton (1960 -) b: 02 Oct 1960

Compelling Journey

.... 5 Anita Floyd (1935 -) b: 02 May 1935 in Cass, Texas, USA

.... + Jerry Wallace Smith m: 27 Jun 1953 in DALLAS TX.

.... 4 Ida Mae Floyd (1913 -) b: 17 Mar 1913 in Cass, Texas, USA

.... + Virgil Windham m: 13 Dec 1929

.... 4 Christene Floyd (1915 - 1976) b: 27 Nov 1915 in Cass, Texas, USA, d: 12 Dec 1976 in Cass, Texas, USA

.... + Charles Spotts m: Titus, Texas, USA

.... 4 Almer Erbirene Floyd (1918 -) b: 23 Feb 1918 in Cass, Texas, USA

.... + Emitchs Smith m: 08 Jul 1934

.... 4 Buddie Floyd (1920 - 1921) b: 17 Jul 1920 in Cass, Texas, USA, d: 23 Feb 1921 in Texas, USA............ 4 Ada Louise Floyd (1922 -) b: 29 Jun 1922

.... + Virgil E. Lewis m: 26 Feb 1962 in Hughes Springs, Cass, Texas, USA

.... 3 Minnie Floyd (1879 -) b: 1879

.... 3 Katie Floyd (1881 -) b: May 1881

.... 3 Willie Victoria Floyd (1890 -) b: 25 Mar 1890

.... 3 Alice Cordelia Floyd (1891 -) b: May 1891

.... 3 John Robert Floyd (1892 -) b: 30 Sep 1892

.... 3 Effie Elena Floyd (1896 -) b: 11 May 1896

.... 2 Andrew Jackson Stubbs (1853 -) b: 21 Oct 1853 in Georgia, USA

2 Cynthia Ann Stubbs (1856 -) b: 07 Sep 1856 in Stone Mountain, GA

+ Noah Lewis Parker (1858 -) b: 1858, m: 28 Jun 1874 in Newton, Georgia, USA

Earl Stubbs

.... 3 Aube Parker (1878 -) b: 1878 in Newton, Georgia, USA

.... 3 Thomas M. Parker (1875 -) b: Sep 1875
....   + Mollie Biddy (1881 -) b: Nov 1881, m: 1897
.... 3 Alice Cordelia Parker (1878 - 1969) b: 02 Feb 1878 in Eastman, Dodge, Georgia, USA, d: 16 Aug 1969 in Hughes Springs, Cass, Texas, USA
....   + Jack Foster (1873 -) b: Sep 1873, m: 1891
.... 4 Harmond Foster (1892 -) b: Nov 1892
.... 4 Emmett Foster (1894 -) b: Jun 1894
.... 4 Luther Foster (1897 -) b: Nov 1897
.... 3 William Lewis Parker (1878 -) b: Jun 1878 in Hughes Springs, Cass, Texas, USA, d: Hughes Springs, Cass, Texas, USA
....   + Katy Bell Williams (1882 -) b: Nov 1882, m: 1898
.... 4 Mariola Parker (1899 -) b: Apr 1899
.... 4 Morris Parker (1902 -) b: 1902
.... 4 Leone Parker (1904 -) b: 1904
....   + Ernest Hall
.... 5 Merlin Carnell Hall
....   + Loyd Wayne Jones
.... 4 Maudie May Parker (1906 -) b: 1906
.... 4 Willie Bell Parker (1908 -) b: 1908
.... 2 James Madison Stubbs (1859 - 1944) b: 23 Mar 1859, d: 20 Apr 1944 in Cass, Texas, USA
....   + Lucy Delula Ivy (1860 - 1933) b: 18 Apr 1860 in Georgia, USA, m:

Compelling Journey

27 Dec 1878 in Newton, Georgia, USA, d: 15 Mar 1933 in Cass, Texas, USA

.... 3 Valary Stubbs (1878 - 1970) b: 05 Nov 1878, d: 1970
.... + Benjamin Weatherby Taylor m: 27 Nov 1899
.... 4 Stella Glyn Taylor (1903 -) b: 23 Apr 1903
.... + Fnu Camp
.... 5 Billy Camp
.... 5 Bobby Joe Camp
.... 5 Glen Dale Camp
.... 5 Marie Camp
.... 4 Mattie Inez Taylor (1905 -) b: 01 Dec 1905
.... 4 James Curtis Taylor (1908 -) b: 01 Mar 1908
.... 4 Era Aline Taylor (1910 -) b: 25 Sep 1910
.... 4 Benjamin Weathreby Taylor JR (1917 -) b: 04 Dec 1917
.... + Lucille Smith (1929 -) b: 21 Jul 1929, m: 13 Aug 1951
.... 5 Ben Wesley Taylor (1952 -) b: 21 Jul 1952
.... + Sonya Lnu (1957 -) b: 10 Nov 1957
.... 6 Benjamin Taylor (1981 -) b: 16 Apr 1981
.... 6 Jessica Anita Marie Taylor (1985 -) b: 16 Apr 1985
.... 5 Glenda Lucille Taylor (1953 -) b: 05 Oct 1953
.... + Reggie Holland
.... 6 Jeremy Nathaniel Holland (1974 -) b: 28 May 1974
.... 6 April Holland (1977 -) b: 23 Apr 1977
.... 6 Matthew Holland (1979 -) b: 31 Aug 1979
.... + Billy Spence
.... 5 Rebecca Valary Taylor (1957 -) b: 29 Sep 1957

Earl Stubbs

.... + Richard Allison
.... 6   Christopher Eric Allison (1975 -) b: 28 Jun 1975
.... + Steve Erwin
.... 4   Royce Allen Taylor (1921 -) b: 19 Nov 1921
.... 3   Walter James Stubbs (1881 - 1973) b: 02 Feb 1881, d: 30 Sep 1973
.... + Augusta Gertrude Mauldin (1885 - 1978) b: 13 Feb 1885, m: 30 Sep 1900, d: 30 Jul 1978
.... 4   Bernice Herschel Stubbs (1901 - 1982) b: 01 Sep 1901, d: 11 Feb 1982
.... + Hattie Mae Ogles (1901 - 1987) b: 29 Aug 1901, m: 14 May 1921, d: 08 Apr 1987
.... 5   Bernice Harlan Stubbs (1922 -) b: 05 Mar 1922
.... 6   Ricky Joe Stubbs (1966 -) b: 21 Feb 1966
.... + Katherine Allday
.... 7   Jody Lynn Stubbs (1971 -) b: 29 Dec 1971
.... 8   Ryne Allen Stubbs (1996 -) b: 15 Dec 1996
.... 8   Layne Elizabeth Stubbs (1999 -) b: 12 Dec 1999
.... 7   Robert Andrew Stubbs (1984 -) b: 04 Oct 1984
.... 7   James Clinton Stubbs (1987 -) b: 07 Sep 1987
.... 5   Billy Ray Stubbs (1929 - 1980) b: 07 Jun 1929, d: 15 Mar 1980
.... 4   Lois Faye Stubbs (1903 -) b: 06 Dec 1903
.... 4   Lula Adelle Stubbs (1907 - 1910) b: 20 May 1907, d: 22 Aug 1910

Compelling Journey

.... 4 Joseph Weldon Stubbs (1909 - 1968) b: 18 Jul 1909, d: 13 Oct 1968
.... + Oneida Kirklan (1914 -) b: 06 Nov 1914, m: 29 Aug 1931 in Texarkana, Miller, Arkansas, USA
.... 5 Troy Dale Stubbs (1935 -) b: 12 Mar 1935
.... + Fnu Lnu
.... 6 Michael Stubbs
.... 6 Jeff Stubbs
.... 6 Steven Stubbs
.... 5 Freddy Carol Stubbs (1940 -) b: 08 May 1940
.... + Fnu Lnu
.... 6 Angia Stubbs
.... 4 Dorthy Mozelle Stubbs (1912 - 1976) b: 27 Mar 1912, d: 05 Jul 1976
.... + Billy Barnwell m: 03 Dec 1933 in Arkansas, USA
.... 5 Billy Ruth Barnwell (1934 -) b: 27 Nov 1934
.... + Fnu Lnu
.... 6 Mike Lnu
.... 6 Chris Lnu
.... 6 Briget Lnu
.... 6 Stephanie Lnu
.... 5 Jerry Judson Barnwell (1944 -) b: 06 Feb 1944
.... + Betty Lnu
.... 6 Kippie Shanay Barnwell
.... 6 Jerry Robert Barnwell
.... 4 Mona Rae Stubbs (1915 -) b: 03 Feb 1915

Earl Stubbs

.... + Ernest Reffer Bradford m: 30 Sep 1931 in Daingerfield, Morris, Texas, USA

.... 5 Peggy Joyce Bradford (1935 -) b: 01 Jul 1935

.... + William Darrell Robertson m: 09 Aug 1951

.... 6 Robert Wayne Robertson (1953 -) b: 24 Apr 1953

.... + Dena Ellen Lofton

.... 7 Dena Di'ann Robertson (1976 -) b: 22 Mar 1976

.... 7 Donita Leigh Robertson (1977 -) b: 25 Oct 1977

.... + Terri Morh m: 18 Mar 1983

.... 7 Sheena Robertson (1987 -) b: 31 Aug 1987

.... 6 Richard Derrell Robertson (1955 -) b: 23 Oct 1955

.... + Donna Kay Furrow m: 18 Mar 1983

.... 7 Carrie Dawn Furrow Robertson

.... 6 Regina Rae Robertson (1957 -) b: 12 Feb 1957

.... + Bobby Glenn Cloud m: 27 Mar 1975

.... 7 James Robert Cloud (1977 -) b: 01 Oct 1977

.... 7 Brody Glen Cloud (1980 -) b: 15 Jul 1980

.... + Robert Calvin Houtchens m: 26 Sep 1961

.... 5 Ernest Doyle Bradford (1938 -) b: 02 Dec 1938

.... + Jerry Colt

.... 6 Roy Dean Bradford (1958 -) b: 23 Jun 1958

.... 6 Katherinne Rena' Bradford (1959 -) b: 31 Jul 1959

.... 6 Robin Gale Bradford (1960 -) b: 09 Aug 1960

.... 5 Larry Winston Bradford (1943 -) b: 24 Apr 1943

.... + Donna West m: 03 Aug 1960

Compelling Journey

.... 6 Randon Lee Bradford (1962 -) b: 11 Aug 1962
.... 6 Redana Lee Bradford (1964 -) b: 27 Aug 1964
.... + Susan Estella Shipley m: 09 Mar 1973
.... 6 Kelly Vaughn Bradford (1987 -) b: 14 Nov 1987
.... + Lamon Smith
.... 6 Benny Jack Bradford (1968 -) b: 09 May 1968
.... 5 Melba Joan Bradford (1945 -) b: 18 Nov 1945
.... + Charles Frank Turner JR m: 06 Mar 1965
.... 6 Stephanie Ann Turner (1966 -) b: 17 Aug 1966
.... 6 Laura Jean Turner (1970 -) b: 21 Feb 1970
.... 5 Pamela Jo Bradford (1952 -) b: 25 Dec 1952
.... + Bobby Frank Golden JR. m: 11 Sep 1971
.... 6 Heather Dawn Golden (1973 -) b: 27 Sep 1973
.... 6 Lesley Nicole Golden (1977 -) b: 21 Apr 1977
.... + Timothy Wayne Broadway m: 25 Oct 1984
.... 6 Amber Rachelle Broadway (1986 -) b: 28 Jun 1986
.... 5 Remona Lisa Bradford (1955 -) b: 05 Dec 1955
.... + Kermit Preston Cherry JR. m: 10 Jun 1977
.... 6 Karisa June Cherry (1982 -) b: 06 Aug 1982
.... 6 Cameron Trey Cherry (1986 -) b: 15 Mar 1986
.... 4 W. J. Stubbs (1915 -) b: 03 Feb 1915
.... + Geneva Burns (- 1980) m: 25 Nov 1954 in Linden, Cass, Texas, USA, d: 17 Nov 1980
.... 4 Thera Maxine Stubbs (1918 -) b: 16 Jan 1918
.... + Ocie Riggins m: 18 May 1940
.... 5 Kay Francis Riggins (1941 -) b: 17 Apr 1941

Earl Stubbs

.... + Fnu Halley
.... 6 Shelley Halley
.... 6 Tony Halley
.... 6 Kim Halley
.... 5 Bobby Glynn Riggins (1944 -) b: 16 Nov 1944
.... + Fnu Lnu
.... 6 Wade Allen Riggins
.... 6 Melissa Gayle Riggins
.... 5 Judy Lynn Riggins (1948 -) b: 18 Mar 1948
.... + Paul Griffin
.... 6 Christy Griffin
.... 6 Teresa Kay Griffin
.... 4 David Quincy Stubbs (1920 - 1951) b: 20 May 1920, d: 20 Aug 1951
.... 4 Frances Laverne Stubbs (1922 -) b: 28 Dec 1922
.... + Weldon Wommack m: 10 Mar 1948 in Texarkana, Miller, Arkansas, USA
.... 5 Francis Lavon Womack (1949 -) b: 01 Feb 1949
.... + Glen Bryant
.... 5 Gayla Diann Womack (1952 -) b: 21 Feb 1952
.... + Jim Masecery
.... 6 Dawn Masecery
.... 6 Shannon Masecerhy
.... 3 Ella Clyde Stubbs (1883 -) b: 07 Jul 1883
.... + Judson Dudley Price
.... 4 Ella Mae Price (1908 - 1982) b: 12 Oct 1908, d: 25 Apr 1982

Compelling Journey

```
..................... + John L Barker m: 1928
................ 3   John Robert Stubbs (1886 - 1887) b: 27 Feb 1886, d: Sep 1887
................ 3   Liller Stubbs (1891 - 1898) b: 25 Dec 1891, d: 07 Jun 1898
                3    Carlton S. Stubbs (1889 - 1966) b: 01 Oct 1892 in Newton,
                     Georgia, USA, d: 17 May 1966
                  + Ada Mae Carurle (1888 - 1987) b: 16 Jan 1888, m: 25 Nov
                     1909, d: 10 Feb 1987
..................... 4   Christine Stubbs (1910 - 1987) b: 14 Nov 1910, d: 22 Mar 1987
..................... + John Crossland (1908 - 1971) b: 22 May 1908, m: 29 Dec 1928, d: 22 Oct 1971
........................ 5  Sherron Crossland (1943 - ) b: 29 Dec 1943
........................ + Johnnie Beckham
........................... 6  Michaele Beckham
........................... 6  Johnnie Beckham
........................... 6  Bridgett Beckham (1968 - ) b: 27 Dec 1968
..................... 4   Lillian Stubbs (1912 - 1988) b: 05 Sep 1912, d: 22 Jan 1988
..................... + Oneal Lee (1909 - 1972) b: 29 Nov 1909, m: 25 Nov 1928, d: 21 Nov 1972
........................ 5  Kenneth Lee (1935 - ) b: 26 Nov 1935
........................ + Mary Lindsey
........................... 6  Lisa Lee
........................... 6  Scott Lee
........................ 5  Doyce Lee (1940 - ) b: 02 Sep 1940
........................ + Phyllis Lnu
........................ 5  Phyllis Lee (1949 - ) b: 28 Sep 1949
```

Earl Stubbs

.... + Tex Clair
.... 6   Paul Clair
.... 6   Charobinette Clair
.... 6   Chase Clair
.... 4   Jewell Stubbs (1915 -) b: 31 Mar 1915
.... + Ray Grubbs
.... + Norris Bigley (1913 - 1938) b: 16 May 1913, m: 02 Nov 1937, d: 26 May 1938....................... 4   Margare Stubbs (1917 -) b: 01 Sep 1917
.... + Louis Bradford
.... + O'Dell Willis (1916 -) b: 28 Mar 1916, m: 06 Jul 1956
.... 4   Madison Stubbs (1920 - 1922) b: 02 Apr 1920, d: 03 Feb 1922
.... 4   Jacqualine Stubbs (1926 -) b: 03 Mar 1926
.... + Eldredge Fleming (1924 -) b: 24 Jun 1924, m: 14 Aug 1946
.... 5   Donna Fleming (1947 -) b: 16 Jun 1947
.... + James Powell
.... 6   Justin Powell
.... 3   Altha Mary Stubbs (1894 - 1902) b: 21 Apr 1894, d: 11 Jun 1902
.... 3   Edgar Stubbs (1897 - 1945) b: 25 May 1897, d: Abt. 1945
.... 3   Marvin Lester Stubbs (1900 - 1976) b: 03 Sep 1900, d: 01 Jan 1976
.... + Willie Gertrude Hampton (1905 - 1936) b: 15 Oct 1905 in Clay, Alabama, USA, m: 12 Aug 1923, d: 09 Jul 1936 in Texarkana, Miller, Arkansas, USA

Compelling Journey

.... 4 Anna Marvalynn Stubbs (1925 -) b: 12 Mar 1925
.... + Blewett Garland Cotton (1917 - 1962) b: 24 Dec 1917, m: 30 Jun 1949, d: 21 Sep 1962
.... 5 Carol Lynn Cotton (1953 -) b: 26 Apr 1953
.... + Gregory Charles Shirley (1952 -) b: 10 Sep 1952, m: 17 May 1975
.... 6 Justin Scott Shirley (1977 -) b: 23 Dec 1977
.... 6 Allison Leigh Shirley (1980 -) b: 23 Sep 1980
.... 5 Gary Blewett Cotton (1958 -) b: 14 Jun 1958
.... + Cindy Kay Oliver (1960 -) b: 23 May 1960
.... 6 Philip Ryan Cotton (1985 -) b: 07 Aug 1985
.... 6 Stephen Mark Cotton (1988 -) b: 13 Apr 1988
.... 4 Dorothy Jean Stubbs (1930 -) b: 02 Apr 1930
.... + Joe Tom Terrell m: 08 Nov 1952
.... 5 Tommy Jack Terrell (1954 - 1994) b: 01 Oct 1954, d: 1994
.... + Terri Lynn Garren (1955 -) b: 27 Apr 1955
.... 4 Earl Wayne Stubbs (1934 -) b: 10 Aug 1934 in Marietta, Cass, Texas, USA
.... + Nancy Lynn Jacobs (1937 -) b: 03 Feb 1937, m: 31 Jul 1954 in Farmersville, Collin, Texas, USA
.... 5 Michael Wayne Stubbs (1957 -) b: 17 Jun 1957
.... + Cindy Louise Near (1961 -) b: 17 Sep 1961, m: 11 Jul 1981
.... 6 Travis Wayne Stubbs (1987 -) b: 11 Mar 1987
.... 6 Jordan William Stubbs (1991 -) b: 16 Aug 1991

Earl Stubbs

.... 5 Mark Alan Stubbs (1960 -) b: 31 Aug 1960
....   + Carolyn Cougar (1961 -) b: 29 Dec 1961, m: 08 Aug 1987
.... 6 Karla Lynn Stubbs (1995 -) b: 16 Feb 1995
.... 6 Jennifer Ellen Stubbs (1995 -) b: 16 Feb 1995
.... 6 Aaron Mark Stubbs (1996 -) b: 15 Nov 1996
....   + Bonnie Dudley
....   + Ollie Knight m: 09 Sep 1933
....   + Annie Richerson m: 13 Dec 1935

FLAT CREEK CEMETERY

Compelling Journey

Part II

The Hampton Journey

**Ephraim Burton Hampton
And wife
Sarah Ruth Peek**

Earl Stubbs

7

The first requisite of a good citizen in this republic of ours is that he/she is able and willing to pull his/her weight—Theodore Roosevelt

ANNA LIZA HERREN HAMPTON

Annie Orlean Hampton Crossland and Milton Hugh Hampton provided most of the family information contained in this section. Annie, my first cousin and the oldest child of my mother's sister, Ruth, compiled the names, birthdates, death dates, and marriage dates in many cases, of the family of our grandmother, Anna Liza Herren Hampton.

Milton Hugh Hampton lived a few miles from me in Naples while I grew up. His daughter, Nancy Jean, was a schoolmate at Pewitt High School. His brother-in-law, Coy Moreland, was a classmate all the way through school. To my knowledge, I never met Hugh.

Hugh's father, Oliver Hampton, was a brother to my grandfather, William Henry Hampton. Since Grandfather

Compelling Journey

Hampton passed almost twenty-five years before my birth, I remained unaware of either Hugh or my great uncle Ollie who lived in my hometown as well.

Hugh journeyed to Alabama and researched our branch of the Hampton clan. Obviously, he found relatives since the information he brought back is quite detailed. I made the same pilgrimage myself, but only found a few gravestones.

I grew up surrounded by my mother's kin, but I met very few and became acquainted with virtually none. A school friend, Franklin Hampton, was very much a part of George Hampton's family. We were unrelated. I was a member of the Ruth Hampton side. Frank attended Hampton family gatherings and related to me tidbits about my kin, but it meant nothing to me since I didn't know any of them.

To the contrary, many members of our mother's family meet each year at the Hampton Reunion. Due to a mean and suspicious nature, Ella Clyde Stubbs Price, my guardian, did not encourage or even allow any contact between my mother's family and me. To her credit, she never spoke ill of Willie Gertrude, but why should she? My mother was not a threat.

I can recall one instance when I visited with my Grandmother Hampton in front of our house in Naples. Later, in 1970, I spent several weeks in the hospital in Garland, Texas. She had family members bring her from East Texas to my room. We had a wonderful visit, one that I cherish to this day. She neared ninety years of age at the time.

Little information on our Hampton ancestors survived. Edward Hampton/Adelia Burton of South Carolina, comprise the first generation Hugh found. Their son Ephraim Burton and his wife Sarah Ruth Peek from Talladega, Alabama, are my great-grandparents. My grandfather, William Henry Hampton, migrated to Omaha in Morris County Texas, from Lineville, Alabama. He married my grandmother, Anna Liza Herren. She was about fourteen. William Henry died of pneumonia on November 28, 1912.

This family suffered as the result of William Henry's untimely death. He was thirty-five at the time. Unable to read or write, Anna was the sole provider for Ruth-14, Nettie-12, Gertrude-7, Wayne-3, Opal-1, and she was pregnant with William, another female, who arrived in 1917.

OMAHA, TEXAS-1900

Compelling Journey

Tragedy followed this family. From left: Nett died at 33, the infant Wade died at 3, Anna, the mother, at 94, Zeala died at 19, Gertrude, my mother, died at 31, William Henry, my grandfather, died at 35, Ruth died at 44, and Lois died at 33. My grandmother, Anna, holding her son Wade, buried everyone in this picture...ES

Anna possessed no skills other than housekeeping, cooking, and caring for her children. During the next few years, she took on the domestic responsibilities of several families to feed her children. One such family was the

Earl Stubbs

Jim Stubbs family. Lucy Stubbs, my paternal grandmother, suffered from dementia. Anna provided her care until she passed, and Jim Stubbs fed her children. Of course, as was usually the case, when Grandmother Stubbs passed, Grandmother Hampton and her children had to seek a position elsewhere. My Grandfather Jim did offer one other alternative. He asked for Anna's hand in marriage, but she declined. Smart woman.

Another important way station in the struggle of this incredible woman was the Ed Storey home. A brief marriage ensued and led to the birth of my uncle, Vernon Storey. He is the only remaining member of his generation, and I visit with him frequently. I love Vernon. He served in World War II moving munitions to the front, and spent much of his adult life as a mechanic. He is ninety-five at this writing and loves to play dominos. Vernon is another family member that I enjoy in my declining years.

Somehow, Anna Hampton survived. Her character represented everything that is decent and honorable in the human existence. She possessed the pioneer spirit in its purest form, and showed a great deal of personal strength in caring for her family during those trying times. The memory of Granny Hampton will always mean the world to me.

8

Those who dream by day are cognizant of many things which escape those who dream only by night.--Edgar Allan Poe

WILLIE GERTRUDE HAMPTON STUBBS

Our mother, Willie Gertrude Hampton, arrived in Lineville, Alabama, in 1905. Since I was an infant when she died in 1936, I have no memories of her. Like a sponge, I soak up any information I can gain about her. As her picture unfolds, I find a source for my own personality. I am quite different from my father and sisters. I suspect that Gerti and I shared much common ground. She loved to write letters.

She wrote the following to Mrs. J. A. Penny, a schoolteacher and friend, in Marietta, Texas. Ester Penny and her husband later provided a home for Gertrude's daughters and my sisters, Lynn and Dorothy Stubbs.

Earl Stubbs

Wednesday Morn.

Dear Mrs. Penny

My heart has been made sad for you and that dear mother of yours for having been called upon to part with so dear a treasure. I'm sure I can't find words to express my love and sympathy for you and your loved ones. But I feel as if I can certainly sympathize with you for I too have had to give

Compelling Journey

up Dear Father and three years later a dear sister, just in the bloom of life eighteen years old she was very dear to us it seemed as if it was more than mother could bear but there is one who helps to bear our sorrows and I'm sure that you will find comfort there. Dear mrs Pinny I have been praying for you in the sad trail and let me refer you to a sweet

Earl Stubbs

chapter in John 14th
I am sure you will
find more komfort
there than I could
ever write on this
paper. You know
Jesus says, "Come unto
me all ye that labor and
are heavy laden and I
will give you rest.
Take my yoke upon you
and learn of me for I am
meek and lowly in
heart and ye shall find
rest unto your souls."
Is not that a
beautiful text?
I am afraid you will

Compelling Journey

not be able to find much comfort in this letter, but I wanted you to know that I have been so sad for you and I only wish I could find words to express my feelings for you. Give my love and sympathy to your mother tho. I ~~am~~ not acquainted with her I feel like to know her would be to love her, because she is your mother. I will go. ~~ours~~ you have my deepest regards your friend
Gertrude Stubbs

Earl Stubbs

This letter written by Willie Gertrude Hampton Stubbs is to her sister Opal. She makes reference to her children Marva (Lynn), Dorothy, her brother Vernon, Christine, Jewell (Marvin's nieces), Ella Price (Marvin's sister) Anna (Her mother), and Lucy Stubbs (Marvin's mother).

Compelling Journey

I could not get a minute ease I thought I was going to cramp to Death for a while but I finally got enough peppermint to stay on my stomach to ease me a little I have been sewing today Ruby was in — is visiting his mother she gave Dorothy Jean 10 pair of little pants and enough cloth to make her two dresses and a pair of bloomers I sure did appreciate them she said her baby had had so many she gave to him he could never wear them out Mother said for me to tell

Earl Stubbs

Compelling Journey

Dorothy Jean ask about you
lots. And Mama wants
me to yell at about writing but
I don't have time to yet for
her. Well Opal I will have to
close now and go to
milk I have to go half
way to Carl's to milk
I will send you all some
peaches if I can get
any when they get ripe
we will soon have watermelons
and cantalopes too.
Well Opal be a good girl
and write to me a little
we have any thing to write
with in that this is my last
stamp and child took
my cent air Arthur
had which was only 3¢ but
that meant a lot to
us well by by lots
of love from Mother & Gertie
ans soon.

Earl Stubbs

Willie Gertrude Hampton Stubbs wrote this card to her brother, Vernon Storey, less than three months before she died in July of 1936.

> Hello Vernon, Old Dear:- 4/ 14/ 36/
> Well you did not get to visit us last week end did you I sure was proud of that picture you sent me it is the best one you ever had made, Did you go up to Ruths to see Mama? I sure do want Mama to come home. and Vernon I want you to come Home as soon as you can I want to help you get mama something for a "Mothers day gift". You save some of your money to get it with so we can get it when you come home again you let me know when you will get to come and I will try to meet you at Queen City. say has A.D. ever got home yet. Pugh is coming this week if he is not already here. Say he is writing to Hollie so that leaves you up against it don,t it. You know Hollie was sick that time you and Wayne was over there, well she has been real bad sick yesterday was the first time she has been to school since you was here. well Vernon I will have to close come firstchance you get Love Gertie

Compelling Journey

Willie Gertrude's sister, Lois, wrote this letter on January 21, 1936. They were both concerned about the health of their mother, Anna, who lived to 93. Both Gertrude and Lois passed away within a year.

9

Life is a thing that mutates without warning, not always in enviable ways--Diane Ackerman

Zelma Ruth Hampton Hampton

**Memories Shared
By
The Children of
George and Ruth Hampton**

As Compiled by

Alma Lavern Hampton Vaughn

**Originally Published by
Brenda Hampton Godwin**

I am certain that before my mother, Willie Gertrude Hampton Stubbs, passed in 1936, I spent quality time with my Aunt Ruth's family, but since I was an infant, I have no recollections of the events. Ruth's son, George Weldon, was the one I knew best,

Compelling Journey

because he was at Naples High School when I started there in the first grade. He kept reminding me of who he was and who I was. Unfortunately, I could only relate to the memory of my sisters who lived a scant nine miles away in Marietta. I visited with them only three or four times while growing up in Naples.

My separation from the Hampton family, for the most part, lay at the feet of my aunt and legal guardian, Ella Clyde Stubbs Price, who grabbed me up at my mother's funeral and never let go. Fearing anything or anyone that would risk losing the replacement for her own infant son who died after a few days of life, she cut me off from the Hamptons, even though they were within easy visiting distance. I recall only one visit from my grandmother, Anna Liza Herren Hampton, while growing up. Ella Clyde did not invite her into our house, but we had a short visit at the car. This visit occurred during the 1940's. I did not see her again until 1970.

That year, I contracted viral pericarditis, a serious infection of the lining of my heart. While in the hospital in Garland, Granny Hampton arranged a visit. She was ninety at the time. We spent forty-five minutes or so together that day. I never saw her again. I consider those moments some of the most important in my life.

Even though I made no real effort to connect with my Hampton relatives over my adult years, I began to form relationships, beginning with Vernon. We lived in Garland at the same time, and he always tuned up our lawn mower. Much later, I began working with Annie on her family tree project. Gradually, I found that these wonderful people were my real family. It is ironic that with two exceptions, my Stubbs cousins have all passed.

Earl Stubbs

Truth be known, there was little warmth given or received over the decades from the Stubbs, and they lost their relevance in my life decades ago with the exception of Rick Stubbs and his family and Ben Taylor and his family. However, my associations with the Hamptons grow stronger as I move from one generation to the next. Having attention deficit disorder made it difficult since my ability to recall the names of people I have met several times is quite limited and embarrassing at the same time. I do the best I can.

Ruth and George's children are the core of the Hamptons of East Texas. As their number succumbed to age, their offspring took up the mantle and held the family together. The primary reasons for this close-knit group stems from their parents. Even my mean-spirited guardian, Ella Price, had nothing but good things to say about Aunt Ruth. After re-reading the magnificent Memory Book produced by Brenda Hampton Godwin, compiled by Lavern Hampton Vaughan from the memories of her brothers and sisters, with additional excerpts from Robert Marlin Hampton, and Evelyn Hampton Jacobs, I cannot conceive of how a set of parents could give more to their family than did George and Ruth. I so admire George who took up the mantle of his wife when she passed to raise and provide for his children.

Compelling Journey

10

Action is character--F. Scott Fitzgerald

MOVING DAY 1938

For several years, we lived on the Milt Heard farm at Cornett. Our brother, Robert (Tuff), drew his first breath there. Vernon came to see him. He got over by the bed in the fireplace room and got a good look at him, and he said he was such a pretty baby.

Papa farmed this land on thirds and fourths. That meant Mr. Heard got 1/3 of the money crops, and 1/4 of the feed crops. Mama and Papa decided we would move to their place at Cross Roads.

We moved in wagons with two mules pulling each wagon. One wagon and team was Papa's and he borrowed one. We think the latter might have belonged to John Betts. Annie and Albert lived on his place and farmed on halves. That meant that John furnished the seed and equipment to farm. They did the work, got half of the harvest, and John got half of the harvest.

The wagons both made more than one trip. The moving started early that morning and lasted all day. In fact, we may not have moved all of our belongings in one day. We moved all of the farm equipment as well as everything in the house. Probably the hardest thing to move was the wood-burning cook stove. We could not move it until Mama cooked for the day and the stove cooled. We didn't have a lot of furniture. We had a safe to keep food in, a cabinet, four cowhide bottom chairs, and a bench. The bench made it possible for all the family members to sit around the table for a meal. Mama and Papa sat on one side in two chairs, two kids sat at each end in a chair, and the rest of us sat on the bench. It was a little crowded, but I don't remember that being a problem, except once when Auvis was about two years old, and he fell off the bench. He hit his head with a snuff glass and cut a gash over his eye. I don't think the glass broke.

Snuff glasses were the only kind of glasses we had. We were happy with them and didn't know there was any other kind. The bench also served as a wash bench on washday. Mama carried it outside and put her tubs on it.

Besides this kitchen furniture, we had three full size beds and a half bed which we called a "little bed". I'm sure we had lots of jars of canned stuff to move and a few clothes. We didn't have a lot of possessions, but moving was still a big job.

The nearest way to the new house was through the woods. It may have been five miles, maybe less. It would have been twice that far or more around the road, so the wagons went through the woods. This meant the wagons had to ford Kelly Creek. The water was low enough it did not get in the wagon bed, but it was down one steep bank and up the other. I don't guess the mules were afraid but the little kids were.

The wagonload that carried the chickens, little kids, and Evelyn got to the house in Cross Roads after the middle of the evening. She was about sixteen years old. 15 or 20 of the hens smothered to death in the move. Evelyn dressed one to cook and threw the rest away. Mama got to the new house about sundown. When she learned about the chickens dying, she gathered them up, and with the help of the family, dressed them, boiled them until tender, probably 3 hours or more, and deboned them. She put them in jars and pressured them. She did all of this after a hard day of moving plus the woodstove had to set up and the stovepipe run through the roof.

Mama never had a doubt about what to do about those chickens. The only way she could keep them from spoiling was to can them. So that is what she did. It took her all night, and she worked by the light of a coal oil lamp. She was fortunate to have an Aladdin lamp, which gave better light than the regular coal oil lamp. That lamp had a mantle that turned to ash after lighting. It was very delicate and would break apart if anyone moved the lamp. Then, we could not use the lamp until we replaced the mantle. (Auvis restored this lamp.) Though Mama had no electricity or refrigeration to help out, she never missed it, because she had never had it.

It was a lot of work to can these chickens, but some of the children remember how good they were when Mama made dumplings, stew, or dressing. She may have made other dishes also.

Maybe we forgot, to some degree, what a job it was to find the jars among the boxes of things just moved. There surely were other hardships and inconveniences, but Mama was not one to waste anything. She didn't consider that it was too hard. She just did it.

Compelling Journey

11

**I have always thought the actions of men the best interpreters of their thoughts--
John Locke**

HOG KILLING DAY

Every year the family killed hogs for meat for the family. We usually killed them in November, but could kill them as late as March. To slaughter hogs, you need a cold, dry day, and, hopefully, no wind. We did this work outside, and a cold wind would make it hard, if not impossible, to do the work. The farmer needed experience to pick such a day. This was before the days of television and electricity so he had no radio for a weather report. The cities and towns had electrical power. The rural areas didn't get electricity until in the 1940's, and many rural families didn't get it until the 50's or 60's.

When Papa made the decision to kill hogs, we usually killed two on the same day. We filled the wash pot with water and built a fire around it. The water had to be the right temperature to make it possible to scrape the hair off the hog. If it was too hot, it would set the hair, and we couldn't get it off. We tested the water by dipping our hands in it. It was the right temperature when someone could dip his or her hand in it three times.

While the water was heating, we dug a slanted hole in the ground, and then we put a barrel in the hole with the lower edge of the front off the barrel even with the ground. They put boards down in front of the barrel. After we completed all of this, and the water was the right temperature, it was time to kill the hog.

Papa shot the hogs with his .22 rifles. That was the only gun Papa had and the only one he needed. When the hog fell, George Weldon and Lawrence jumped over the pen. Each grabbed a front leg and turned the hog on its back. Then, one would stick a butcher knife in its jugular vein so its blood would drain out. They put the hog on a slide hitched to a horse and drug it to the barrel. They put it in the barrel, back end first, and poured the water over it. When they could pull the hair off easily, it was ready to scrape. They put it on the boards and all who could get around it, scraped the hair off with a knife. If the hog was too big to go in the barrel, they put him on the boards, lay tow sacks on him, and poured water on him until he was ready to scrape. When they scraped the hair off, they slit the skin on the back legs, and hooked the ends of a single tree under the tendons in the legs. (A single tree is a piece of wood about two feet long with metal pieces on each end. Farmers use it to hitch a mule or horse to a plow, wagon, or slide.) The workers pulled the single tree up into a tree with a rope, thus hanging the hog off the ground. They poured water on the hog and washed it, and then they split it open and let all its insides fall into a tub. Then they poured water inside the hog to wash it.

They separated the insides that were in the tub. They took out the heart, liver, and melt (the spleen). They gave the melt to the kids who would roast the melt over a fire and eat it. Some people cleaned the entrails and ate them, but our family did not.

Our women took the entrails and stripped the fat off them to make lard. This was a dirty job. Sometimes you would burst a gut. When this happened, you had to tie it off. We saved all of this fat, plus any trimmed off the meat, and rendered lard out of it. ,

Meanwhile, the men put the hog on a table and cut it into hams, shoulders, middlings, pork chops, and ribs. The trimmings from these were ground into sausage. They had to use the right proportion of lean and fat meat to make the sausage cook and taste right. After the sausage was ground, Papa would season it with sugar cure, salt, sage, and pepper. Mama would cook one for him to see if he needed to add more seasoning. Early in the year, Mama would make small, long sacks out of flour sacks and stuff them full of sausage. We hung them in the smoke house and used them as needed. If the weather got too warm, Mama would fry the sausage, pour grease over them, and seal them in jars. We could eat these anytime, as they would keep all year like this.

Papa sugar cured the hams and shoulders. We ate them first as they did not keep as well as the middlings. We put the middlings in a box and covered them with salt. They would keep like this until used. We made bacon from middlings.

On the day we killed the hogs, we cooked tender loins and sausage for supper.

Hog killing day was a full day of hard work for all the family. Sometimes a neighbor would help, and we gave them a portion of the meat to show appreciation.

The killing of the hogs made it necessary to do other things. Soon after we processed the hogs, we rendered the lard ... usually the next day. The fat that was stripped from the insides of the hog and entrails (this was sometimes cooked separately), and the other fat that was trimmed from it was put in the wash pot. First, we cleaned the inside of the wash pot. We built a fire around the pot, and we cooked the meat to separate out the grease. We stirred the contents of the pot occasionally with a hickory stick to keep the meat from burning. We called the remains of the meat cracklings after we cooked the grease out. Then, we dipped out the cracklings and put them in a cornmeal sack to let the grease drip out. When they were cool enough not to burn your hands, we squeezed the grease out by twisting the sack with a

Compelling Journey

homemade tool made with two boards hinged together. We opened the two boards, lay the sack between them, and pressed the grease out in a dishpan. We stored this lard and that in the pot in 5-gallon cans. We used the lard for seasoning vegetables, frying chickens, potatoes, etc., and for piecrust. We would grind up a few cracklings and use them to make crackling bread, but we used most to make soap.

To make lye soap, Mama put water in the pot and built a fire around it. When the water got hot, she added one or two cans of Eagle lye and stirred the pot with a stick until it dissolved. She was careful not to get the lye on her or breathe the fumes from it. She usually used a handle cut from a worn-out broom for a stick. We called it a punching stick because we used it to punch down clothes when we boiled them in the pot. Next, she added her pigskins and cracklings. She cooked and stirred them until the lye ate them up. She might add more water so that when she finished the soap, she would have more than half a pot full. When the fire went out, she would turn a tub over it so nothing would get in. The next day, she cut the soap into bars, took them out of the pot, and stored them for use as needed to wash clothes, dishes, and hair. We bought hand soap to wash hands and feet and to take our weekly bath.

12

**Life is one long process of getting tired--
Samuel Butler**

WASH DAY

Washday needed to be a sunny day since it took most of the day to do this job. We moved the bench from the eating table outside to hold two washtubs. We filled them with water. One of the kids or Papa would draw all this water from the well for Mama. She cut up lye soap in the wash pot, and built a fire around it to boil the water. The wood for the wash pot was usually tree tops drug up from the woods where we cut firewood for the cook stove or fireplace.

Mama sorted the white clothes, colored (wearing) clothes, and overalls into piles. She put the white clothes in a tub and scrubbed them with a rub board and lye soap to get out stains and dirt. Then, she put them in the pot to boil. Meantime, she got the next pot full ready. When the clothes had boiled awhile, she lifted them out of the pot with the punching stick and put them in a tub.

Compelling Journey

Next, we rinsed that batch through two waters and hung them on a line. The clothesline was wire stretched between two poles, and it had a pole to prop it up in the middle. This pole lowered the line to hang the clothes then prop the line higher for them to dry. The line would not hold near all the clothes, so we hung the towels, washrags, underwear, and other things on the barbwire fence that kept the cattle out of the yard.

We did not boil the good clothes that we wore to church, school, and wherever we went. We scrubbed them on the rub board, rinsed and starched them, and hung them out to dry. We tried to hang the colored ones in the shade and brought them in as soon as they were dry to keep the sun from fading them. We made the starch by boiling water on the wood cook stove and adding a paste made from cold water and Faultless starch. We bought the starch.

We washed the work clothes such as overalls, jumpers, and chambray shirts last.

This was before the days of bleach, but the lye soap and sunshine did a good job of helping keep the clothes white, but Mama put bluing in her rinse water to whiten the clothes also.

When she finished washing, she sometimes used the water to scrub and rinse the kitchen floor. Pine planks made up the floors, and we cleaned them by pouring on water then scrubbing them with a broom. Then, she rinsed and swept the water off. Sometimes, we used an old pair of overalls to dry off the excess water. Then, everyone stayed out of the kitchen until the floor dried.

Washday was a long, hard job but in about 1936 or 37 it got a little easier. Mama got a gasoline-engine washing machine. She bought it from Alvin Irving. Papa had a feed grinder, and he traded it for the washing machine. Washday was still a big job, but easier than before. We filled the wash pot with water, heated it, and put it into the washing machine. Starting with the white clothes, we washed a load at a time in the machine. After the first load washed, Mama ran those through the wringer into the first rinse tub. She put another load into the washer while she rinsed the first load and hung them out. She changed the rinse water often. We changed the first water and moved the second rinse to the first. The washing machine eliminated boiling the clothes in the wash pot. It shortened the washday by several hours and was much easier on Mama. Sometimes the hardest thing to do on washday was to get the machine started. It had a kick lever to start it and sometimes it took a while. Another big job followed when we finished the washing.

13

In this theater of man's life, it is reserved only for God and for angels to be lookers-on-
-Sir Francis Bacon

IRONING CLOTHES

We had to iron all the clothes we wore to school and other places. This was before the days of perma-press, and they wrinkled while drying. We could iron on any day but Sunday. It helped if it was a sunny day, as you had better light to see. We always ironed by daylight since we had no electric lights, and the lamp could not be put in a good place to help with this.

Early on ironing day, we cleaned off the table and wiped it clean. Then, we laid out the clothes on the table, one at a time, and sprinkled them with water. It helped if the water was warm, but it didn't have to be. Sometimes, we put water in a jar and punched holes in the lid to sprinkle the clothes. Sometimes, we sprinkled by getting water in our hands and sprinkling it on the clothes. After we sprinkled each piece, we rolled them up in a folded sheet. After we sprinkled all of the clothes, we rolled them together in the sheet and allowed them to set two or three hours to get uniformly moist so they would not have dry spots and wet spots. Then, we ironed them.

The ironing board was padded. We turned two chairs back to back to keep them from falling over. We put the ironing on these chairs and the other end on the foot of the bed in the fireplace room. Mama had three flat irons ... one small, one medium, and one large. We heated them in the fireplace or on the wood cook stove. When we started to iron, we had to wipe the smut of the iron first and then iron the garment. When the iron began to cool, we put it back in the fire, got another, and wiped the smut off it. Ironing for our big family was usually an all day job and a very hard one too. In later years, Mama got a gasoline iron. That iron didn't get smutty. It was a great improvement over heating the flat irons in the fireplace or on the cook stove. Ironing was still a big job, but not as hard as before. In later years, we kids learned to appreciate electric irons and then permanent press.

14

Character is like a tree and reputation like its shadow. The shadow is what we think of it; the tree is the real thing--Abraham Lincoln

CANNING

Every year when the vegetables were mature or ripe, Mama canned them to feed her family during the winter when there was nothing growing to eat. Though all the family helped, the main responsibility was on her shoulders. She would always try to fill all her jars and usually canned at least four hundred jars a year. She never had a good place to keep her canned goods and empty jars until 1939. That was the year she got a freestanding pantry built. She was so proud. At the same time, she got a freestanding clothes closet built to hang our good clothes in. The closet was probably four feet wide, but it had enough room to hang all the good clothes for our large family.

Earl Stubbs

One year, the family lived near Mr. Andy Long and family. He had a lot of green beans, and he wanted Mama to pick them. She did and canned 36 ½-gallon jars.

When berries got ripe, Papa and the kids would take several one-gallon syrup buckets and go to the woods to pick berries. The briars stuck us, and chiggers covered us. When we got home, someone had to pick the chiggers off you. Meanwhile Mama stayed at the house and got things ready to can the berries. She cleaned the kitchen after breakfast, strained the milk, cleaned up after that, and got dinner started. Usually, the kids washed the jars the day before. Then, we washed the berries in the washtubs through two or three waters. Next, we heated the berries in water on the wood stove and sealed them in quart jars. We used the berries for cobblers or jam, or sometimes we ate them with cake or whipped cream.

Mama helped pick the beans when they were ready to can. The kids could not always tell which ones were ready to pick. After we picked them, everyone helped shell or snap them. Those had to be pressure-cooked.

Mama usually bought peaches and apples. She canned some in quart jars and dried some. To dry them, she sliced them thin and spread them out in the sun until they dried. She had to protect them from chickens and flies to do this. Someone would usually give her pears, and she made preserves from those.

Mama and Papa gathered wild plums, grapes, and muscadine. She made jelly from them. She washed and cooked the grapes and plums. Then, she strained the juice through a meal sack to make the jelly. Sometimes, she made a cobbler out of the plums. She popped the muscadines open; put the plummies in one pan, and the hulls in another. She cooked them separately, made jelly from the juice, but she canned some of the hulls to make cobblers. She ground up some hulls to use, instead of raisins, to go in mincemeat.

She made mincemeat at hog killing time. She used a little of the meat from the hogs head and feet and a lot of fruit. Sometimes she used dried fruit. She used apples, peaches, and raisins. We ate the mincemeat on buttered biscuits, or made it into pies. She made a custard pie and added mincemeat to it in a crust made from hog lard and flour.

Canning corn was a big job. After we gathered it from the field, we shucked and silked the ears. We silked them with an old toothbrush. I'm sure we left a few silks on it, but they didn't hurt the taste. After we silked it, we put the ears in a tub of water. Those cutting it off the cob took it from the tub and cut it with a sharp knife into a dishpan. When they get a dishpan full, we brought it to a boil on the stove. We added water to make the right consistency. When it began boiling, we put it in the cans. We handled those hot cans with rags to keep from getting burned. We sealed the cans, put them in the cooker, and pressured them at 10 pounds for an hour. When we

Earl Stubbs

finished the cooking, we let the steam off, opened the cooker, and emptied it for the next load.

We usually canned corn in tin cans. We used #2 cans that would hold about sixteen ounces. Mama had a can sealer, and the Cornett community had a cooker that people could use. Mama had a cooker too, but when canning corn, it was real handy to have two. Usually, the neighbors would help each other on corn canning day. This was field corn; no one raised sweet corn back then. One day, our family, and the Claude Eaton family helped Mrs. Nanny Boone (Mrs. John Boone) can corn. There were probably about 15 grown-ups and some kids there. Mrs. Boone fixed dinner for all the helpers. Someone mentioned that we didn't have corn for dinner. She replied, "I kept thinking I'd have a piece of a can left over, but I never did." I bet that bunch could have eaten several cans.

Sometimes, Mama canned little potatoes. When they dug them, she scraped the little ones and canned them in quart jars to have when all the others were gone.

She always canned lots of tomatoes in Y2 gallon jars and lots of peas. She worked hard to put up food for the family when there was none in the garden.

Mama not only canned for her own family, but when there was a need, she helped others also. One time, Nolan and Mary Annie Caldwell were canning in cans. Annie Mae Smith was going to seal the cans for them, but her sealer wouldn't work. They came to get Mama to

Compelling Journey

bring her sealer and seal the cans. Mama had just got dinner ready; she had her plate filled ready to eat. She left her food and went right away, as they needed to get the cans sealed as soon as possible. She was always ready to help when there was a need.

When canning in glass jars, the pressure had to go down by itself. Sometimes, it would be after nightfall before the last cooker finished. When we finished the cooking, we had to remove the cooker from the stove. We could not turn off the wood stove as our stoves today. Those cookers were heavy as they contained two or three layers of cans amounting to twenty or more cans in one cooker.

Earl Stubbs

15

They say that blood is thicker than water. Maybe that's why we battle our own with more energy and gusto than we would ever expend on strangers--David Assael

OCCUPATION

Papa was a farmer. This is how he made a living for his family. Mama was a farmer's wife. She helped him in whatever way she could. All the family worked together to raise and gather the crops.

In about 1935, Papa got sick and had to go to the Veterans Hospital in Fayetteville, Arkansas. Mama and Morris took the responsibility of getting the crop in that year. The bigger kids helped, and Annie took over the cooking and care of the little kids.

Mama and Papa milked about 15 cows. These were straight run, not dairy. I'm sure some of the older children helped with the milking. Mama wanted to sell the cream off the milk. While Papa was in the hospital, she sold a cow and bought a milk cream separator. She

Compelling Journey

sold the cow to John Betts. He and Claude Eaton came to talk to Mama about the cow. Mama was in the field plowing with a scratcher. The Bermuda grass was very bad. While she talked with John about the cow, Claude made a round with the scratcher. He was so exhausted he only made one round. Mama did what was necessary to get that crop planted.

Mama got her separator. When we finished milking, we strained the milk into the separator. When we turned the handle, the cream came out one spout and milk called blue john came out the other. We fed the blue john to the hogs. It would probably compare to the 2 % milk bought in the stores today.

One of the best cotton crops Papa made was in 1936. He made 18 bales of cotton that year. He paid the kids 50 cents a hundred to pick. He didn't usually pay us. We had what we needed, and we picked anyway. Mama and Papa taught us all to work together to get done what had to be done. I, Lavern, was four years old, and Mama made me a cotton sack out of a meal sack. It *might* hold 10 pounds of cotton. Papa told me he would give me a nickel if I would fill it up. I got it full, but I remember that Papa put several hands full of cotton in my sack. I went with Morris when he carried the bale of cotton to the gin. He stopped at Herbert Arnold's store and let me spend my nickel. I bought a peanut patty. It was so big, I could not eat it all, but Morris helped me eat it.

Earl Stubbs

Evelyn and Jean spent some of their money for clothes. Mama sent an order to Sears Roebuck for pajamas for Jean. She ordered Jean a pair of red overalls and Evelyn a pair of blue ones. Jean was going to wear hers to the county meet at Linden. She was going to play baseball, but she fell and hurt her hip and didn't get to go. Her overalls went though. Her friend, Christine Vaughan, wore them. Her dad wouldn't let her wear overalls, but he wasn't at the county meet.

Mama thought tomatoes was a good idea for a money crop. She encouraged Papa to plant them for the market. Early in the year, probably about February Papa sprouted his seed. He put them in a tow sack, wet it, and put it under the heater to sprout them. Meantime, he built a hot bed to plant them in. This was dirt, framed in boards. It was probably three or four feet wide and about eight or ten feet long. He ran a tunnel down the center of the frame. He built a fire at one end and the heat would travel through the tunnel and keep the ground warm for his seed. This was where he planted his sprouted seed and let them grow until they were about four inches high. Then, he moved them to a cold frame. The cold frame was bigger than the hot bed and did not have the tunnel. He set the plants in the cold frame about five or six inches apart. He marked his rows in the cold frame with a rake. He put corncobs on the tines of the rake about five or seven inches apart, then he marked the rows both ways, to form squares. The plants were set in the middle of the

Compelling Journey

square. When he removed them from the cold frame and set them in the field, he cut them out in squares, leaving the dirt around the plant. Papa put those on the slide, hauled them to the field, and set them out in rows.

After the plants started producing, we picked some of these tomatoes green and sold them in DeKalb. The ripe tomatoes went to a cannery in Atlanta. They furnished the baskets, and sent a truck to pick up the tomatoes. They had to be good with no blemishes. Of course, Mama could not can tomatoes that had a blemish either, but she and Mrs. Lena Wellborn tried to cook all of these. They had enough for the community.

Another crop we planted was soybeans. Mama cooked some of these, but the family didn't like them. We grew watermelons as well. Besides the money crops, Mama always had a garden. It furnished us with plenty of vegetables to eat and can for later use.

She also had chickens. She raised some for fryers and some for making dressing, dumplings, and stew. She also had laying hens that furnished all the eggs for the family. She sold the extra eggs and bought what she needed.

We didn't buy much but the necessities. We had to buy coal oil for the lamp and to start a fire in the stove. It was 10 cents a gallon. She bought her flour, salt, sugar, soda, and baking powder. Sometimes she bought corn meal, and sometimes we had it ground. She might buy soap. The flour, meal, salt, and sugar came in cloth bags, which she used for many things.

Earl Stubbs

Sometime Mama sold butter. She put the milk in a churn to clabber. When it was clabbered, we churned it until the cream turned to butter. We put the butter into a bowl and beat the milk out of it. Then we washed and salted the butter. If she was going to sell it, she packed it into a butter mold that measured a pound. We left what we used at home in a bowl.

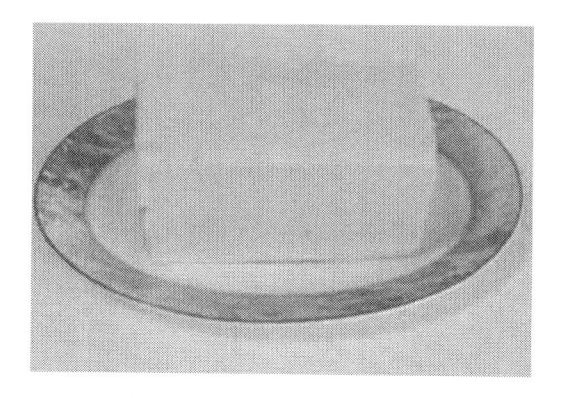

16

**Academic and aristocratic people live in such an uncommon atmosphere that common sense can rarely reach them--
Samuel Butler**

Daily Chores

The day began early on the farm. In the winter, Papa got up and built a fire in the cook stove and one in the heater or fireplace, depending on the house we lived in. Then, Mama would get up, and they fixed breakfast before daylight. Mama always made biscuits for breakfast. She had a big pan of flour. She made a well in this flour and poured her buttermilk in. She measured her salt, soda, and baking powder in her hand and added them to the milk. She put a little shortening in, mixed it up, and mixed the flour in with her hand. She pinched the biscuits off with her fingers and flipped them in grease that she melted in her baking pan. They would all be the same size. Then, she baked the biscuits in the woodstove. It took a lot of biscuits to feed Mama's family.

Earl Stubbs

The pan held 15 or 20, and she made two of these each morning. Morris, Carl, and Mayo could eat this many by themselves.

While Mama made biscuits, Papa cooked the meat from the hogs he had slaughtered. Sometimes he cooked ham or bacon, but usually he cooked sausage. When he cooked ham, he made what he called gravy. When he finished cooking the ham, he poured out most of the grease, then added water to the skillet and rinsed out the skillet. We ate this with our ham and syrup.

Sometimes Papa cooked oatmeal and sometimes he made sugar syrup. He made sugar syrup special by browning the sugar in an iron skillet, then adding water. If he made it plain, he added a little vanilla flavoring. We usually had syrup of some kind to go with our biscuits. Sometimes we had sorghum syrup. Papa raised the sorghum, and they cooked it off on Uncle Pete's syrup mill. A few times, we had ribbon cane syrup from this same method. Mostly, we had Blackburn's syrup, bought from the country store. That would be Ernest Hall's store, when we lived at Cross Roads. When we lived at Cornett, it would be Olin McCord or Herbert Arnold's store. We always had plenty of butter for our biscuits from the cows Mama and Papa milked. Mama and Papa had coffee for breakfast. Papa would perk it on the stove. The kids could have milk, but usually did not drink anything.

If we had not washed the dishes the night before, Papa washed them while Mama fixed breakfast. He had

Compelling Journey

to wash them before we could eat, because we only had enough dishes for one meal.

When breakfast was nearly ready, Papa called the kids. He didn't have to call twice. We all knew when Papa spoke we better listen. We cooked and ate breakfast by the light of a coal oil lamp. About 1935 or 1936, Mama got an Aladdin lamp that gave a better light. It also got pretty warm. Once it was sitting on the dresser. Once we pushed the lamp back close to the mirror and became so hot, it cracked the mirror. We only had this one mirror, so from that time on, we had one mirror, cracked from top to bottom.

After breakfast, at about daylight, we had to care for the livestock. Mama, Papa, and the older kids helped milk the cows. Sometimes, we fed the cows while we milked them. Sometimes, we let the calf suck a little, and then tied the calf off while we milked the cow. They always carried water in the bucket to wash the cow's teats before they started milking. When we finished the milking, Mama carried it to the house and strained it into buckets or churns. We drank some as sweet milk, or we used it for cooking. Some clabbered to churn for butter and buttermilk.

Afterwards, she had a big mess to clean up. She strained the milk through a meal sack. She washed this through two or three clean waters, and then hung it to dry. She washed all of the milk buckets as well as the breakfast dishes. We drew the water from the well with a bucket on a rope and pulley, and brought one bucket at time into the house. We had a water bucket that sat on a shelf. Often, it was made of wood. A dipper was in this bucket to dip out water to use and drink. Everyone drank from this dipper. A wash pan and soap also sat on the shelf with the water, and a towel made from a fertilizer sack hung on a nail nearby. Everyone would wash their face and hands here, then dash the water out the back door. We washed our feet in this wash pan every night. Sometimes, we washed this pan in the dishpan after all the dishes.

Papa and the boys took care of the other animals. After we milked the cows, we turned them out of the pen into the pasture to graze the grass all day. They came up at milking time, or we would drive them up to the pen or barn. At night, we milked them again.

We fed the horses, mules and hogs corn raised on the farm. Papa usually had a crib full of corn at the beginning of winter. We fed the hogs slop. We kept a 5-gallon bucket in the kitchen and poured dishwater in it. Sometimes, we added shorts, a bought feed, and poured it into the trough. They ate it all. We gave most table scraps to the dog.

After Mama cleaned the kitchen and got the kids off to school, depending of the time of year, she sometimes had a little free time to do things she wanted to do or needed to do. She would piece quilts or sew. She had a Singer treadle sewing machine, and she used it to make many

Compelling Journey

garments. She made all of her clothes and the kids clothes including underwear. The boys bought overalls. She sewed for people in the community, especially if their mother had died or if they just had a need. She never charged anything or expected anything in return. She didn't have any dress patterns. She could look at a dress in the catalog and make a dress like it. I think she cut her patterns from newspaper. She never had any straight pins. She would put a glass or knife on her pattern to hold it in place on the material.

When Mama cooked dinner, she cooked enough for supper. This was great in the summer, as she didn't have to heat up the stove again. It made the house hotter in the summer. The only way we had to cool the house was to open all the doors and windows and let the summer heat, flies, and mosquitoes in. We often had cornbread and buttermilk for supper. It doesn't get any better than that.

We washed the dishes three times a day so they would be ready for the next meal. Sometimes, we left the supper dishes and washed them before breakfast. When we did this, we always turned our glasses up side down in our plates so it would not dry out and be hard to wash.

After supper, Mama liked to play 42 with the kids. Everyone was probably in bed by 8 o'clock. The next day started by 5 a.m. at least. It also ended early, so it could start early the next day.

Earl Stubbs

17

History teaches us that men and nations behave wisely once they have exhausted all other alternatives--Abba Eban

ODDS & ENDS

This was back in the days before television, and very few people had a radio. If they had one, they were picky about what they listened to, as they had to make the battery last as long as possible. The young people had to entertain themselves. One of the ways we did this was to spend the night with each other. Sometimes, a visitor would have the itch. (Impetigo) Some people seemed to keep the itch, and it was very hard to cure. When a visitor with the itch stayed the night, the family got it. Mama's family didn't "keep" the itch. She saw to that. Sometimes she boiled polk root and those with the itch would bathe in it. It would break them out and set them on fire, but I guess it killed the itch mites. It nearly killed the kids. There was a medicine called Red Pacific that was supposed to cure the itch. It broke the kids out also.

Compelling Journey

Sometimes, Mama mixed sulfur and hog lard. She put this on the itchy places. I don't know if it got rid of the itch, but it sure didn't smell very good. In later years, Aunt Opal brought us some scabola salve. This was supposed to cure the itch, and I guess it did. Whatever it took, Mama didn't quit until she got us cured.

Another big problem was lice. When we got lice, Mama was just as diligent to get rid of them. She washed our hair in coal oil. She combed them out of our hair with a fine comb. Whatever she had to do, she did. There were no drug store remedies available that we knew of. When she got the kids cured, she tackled the clothing. She washed the sheets, towels, and wearing clothes. She did this with the rub board, lye soap, the wash pot, and plenty of water drawn the hard way from the well.

Mama hated whiskey. About 1929, Jean heard Mama talking about how she hated whiskey. Papa came in one day with a pint of whiskey. She told him that the first drink he took out of that bottle, she was gone. She put it up in the cabinet and used it for medicine. Papa never brought whiskey home after that.

About the same time, a lot of Papa's people visited. The family lived at Cornett near the store. The men were out under the big magnolia tree, and the women were in the house. Jean was outside watching the men. She was three or four years old. Uncle Mock had a bottle of whiskey and he passed it around. When it came to Papa, he took a drink. Jean ran into the house and told Mama.

Earl Stubbs

Mama sewed for everybody. She made some clothes for Mrs. Wallace, a schoolteacher, before Jean started to school. Jean didn't remember if she received pay for it, but I don't think she did.

One time, Mama got Mr. Wynnegar to take some pictures of us. She made us some new clothes for the pictures. She made Tuff a little suit with shorts and a shirt out of fertilizer sacks. They were real cute. Tuff was about three years old. This was when we lived on the Heard place at Cornett. Sometimes, before we took the pictures, Mama made Annie a suit out of fertilizer sacks. It was really pretty. It would have to be for Annie to wear it.

Fertilizer sacks made a lot of things besides clothes. They made sheets, pillowcases, towels, dishtowels, aprons, quilt linings, quilt pieces, and dresser scarves. She also made luncheon cloths. There was a lot of work involved in getting them ready to use. They had words printed in the material. To get these letters out, she wet them and soaped them down with lye soap. She let them soak a while, and then she scrubbed them on the rub board. Maybe she did something else to them, but, eventually, she hung them out in the sunshine. When she got through with them, they would be pretty and white with every trace of the letters gone. If Mama wanted a different color, she just dyed some of the sacks. The material was very good and lasted well.

Compelling Journey

Flour started coming in printed sacks. These made nice blouses and other things.

Mama didn't charge people for sewing for them. She sewed for whoever asked her. She made a dress for Bea, a black lady. Mama asked her how she wanted it made. Bea answered, "I don't care Mrs. Ruth, just so it's short and tight and has something flapping." The style was with a big handkerchief to flap.

Mama made Annie's clothes when she got married. She made a blue crepe dress and a royal blue long coat and skirt. A few years later, when Annie needed one, she made her a maternity dress. She bought some wine silk material with white polka dots and made her a dress.

Mama would darn the socks when they got a hole in the heel. She would put a snuff glass down in the sock and patch the hole. The snuff glass held the sock in place while she sewed.

She found time to piece lots of quilts from her scraps. She probably did that mostly in the winter, when there was no garden or crop. When she died, she had enough tops pieced for all of us kids to have one.

When she quilted a quilt, she carded her bats from her own cotton to make the filler. She had to quilt these very close as cotton will come apart and knot up when washed. The polyester battings of today are a great improvement over the real thing.

When Mama saw a need, she did something about it. Some of us might say, "Somebody should do something about that," but not her. She was "somebody" and she took care of it.

When the peas dried in the field, we picked them, let them lay out in the sun to get brittle, then we put them in a sack, and beat them with a stick to break the hulls to pieces. This was the way we thrashed them. Then, we poured them from a pan into a tub. The peas fell into the tub, and the hulls chaff blew away. Mama gave these peas to people who had no food. She also gave them milk and butter. Jean remembered that Jackie Wilson, or it may have been Montie Mae Motley, would have starved to death, if Mama hadn't helped her.

One time at Christmas, Mama and Papa went to town in Hughes Springs. They bought some fruit, among other things. Mama saw Bassie Kato's kids on the street. They were dirty and hungry. She gave them some fruit to eat. She said she would have bought them some soap, but she was afraid it would hurt their feelings.

One time, Mama fed Montie Mae Motley and her kids, while Jake was gone. He was gone a month, hunting a job.

When anyone got sick, Mama would go. Mrs. Nanny Boone got sick one time, and Mama went to see her. Mrs. Boone said, "I knew you would come." The next time she got sick, she died. Mama went, but she was gone when Mama got there.

Compelling Journey

Mama went when Dan Boone and his wife's baby was born. That was a sad day for everybody. The baby was stillborn. The mother, Florence Barmet Boone, also died.

Mama had kids at home, but she was able to go when there was a need. Annie cared for her little brothers and sisters. When people needed food, Mama usually sent it to them by some of the kids.

When we were kids, there were two churches at Cornett. One Sunday, we went to the Methodist church and the next Sunday to the Baptist church. Only one church had services on any given Sunday. Mama and Papa didn't always go to church, but the kids went. We walked. It was probably more than a mile, but most people walked everywhere they went, or rode in a wagon pulled by mules or horses. Not many people had cars in those days.

Annie remembers Mama going to church with the family. Mama liked to sing. When they asked for a choir, she would go up and sing in the choir. Mama could sing and she could yodel too. She didn't yodel in church, but she yodeled going to milk or coming back to the house from the cow pen. Bet those cows enjoyed it. Also the neighbors and her family, but Mama must have enjoyed it most of all.

Mama always saw that her family had plenty to eat. She was good at trying something different. Some things she cooked didn't go over too well, so she only tried these once. Some of the things she cooked "once" were a coon,

Earl Stubbs

a possum, and a goose. A hawk stew was just like chicken stew.

For Christmas, she cooked a ham from the hog Papa killed. She would make chicken and dressing. Several days before she was ready to do this, we caught the chicken or chickens they planned to kill, and penned them. Mama kept them fed and watered. If she killed them Christmas Eve, she cooked them, but kept the meat cool. That time of year, temperature was usually not a problem. The whole house, for the most part, felt like a freezer. At a warmer time of the year, cooked chicken would sometimes be put in a bucket and let down in the well to keep it from spoiling.

One year Mama made a pound cake. She cooked it in a small aluminum dishpan in the oven of the wood stove. She usually made at least three or four cakes for Christmas. One of the cakes was a hickory nut cake. They were so good, but it took a lot of time and patience to pick out the hickory nuts. You could never get all the hulls out so someone always got a hull in their piece of cake. She would sometimes put a cake or two on the mantle over the fireplace. I guess that was so Santa could get a slice or two.

Mama made teacakes for school lunches. She put them in a meal sack and hung them up in a bucket. She put icing between two cookies and made a cookie sandwich. This was a special treat. In those days, all the kids carried their lunch to school. There were no hot

Compelling Journey

lunches back then. They carried what they had on the farm such as boiled eggs or egg sandwiches made with biscuits, sausage, or ham. Sometimes we had peanut butter and crackers bought from the store. We often paid for the crackers with eggs from the yard.

In 1935, Mama and Papa planted a big turnip patch in the woods. They made lots of turnips and picked a wagonload. They bedded them down (buried them) to keep them from freezing. Carrie Barnett and Anna Crossland (sisters) would come and help Mama quilt. Mama would give them some turnips.

Martha, a black lady that lived close to Kelly Creek, would come and churn for Mama. Mama would give her milk, butter, and vegetables. One day, Martha went through the tomato patch and picked some tomatoes as she went home. She lost her glasses, came back to the house, and told Mama. Mama sent Lavern and maybe Tuff to help find them. They looked and looked, but never found them. Finally, Lavern saw them on the top of her head, but she didn't know those were the ones lost. She thought Martha knew they were there. Later, after Martha got home, she found them on the top of her head.

After Mama died and Evelyn had married, Papa would get Jean up to help cook breakfast. We didn't have a clock, but Papa could tell about what time it was by looking at the stars. One morning it was cloudy and he could not see the stars, but he thought it was time to get up, so he got Jean up, and she cooked breakfast. Then

Earl Stubbs

Papa decided it was too early and did not wake the kids. It must have been about midnight. He got a clock after that.

When Jean was little, she went to the cow pen with Mama and Papa and watched them milk. Mama asked her if she wanted to milk. She said yes. She tried it, but she couldn't milk very well. When she got older, she learned, like the rest of the kids. When we got old enough, we all helped with the work.

Mama and Papa always worked well together. We never heard any fussing, cursing, or raised voices from them. If they had any disagreements, it was between them privately. I don't think any of their ten children lived up to this example they lived before us.

Mama always cared for her family. When Willie was a young girl, she had gone home from school. Mama saw two girls come by with switches. She asked them where they were going. They said, "We're going to get Willie. She's gonna get a whipping." Mama told them, "Willie's at home and you two ought to be home." They went home. Then the teacher, Ed Shaddix, came by. When Mama got through talking to him, he went home too.

Sometime after Wade was born, Grandpa William was digging a well. Two white doves flew out to the well. Grandpa said, "One was for Wade and the other for him." Wade was the first son born to them. They had six girls before him.

Compelling Journey

Grandpa's brother, Oliver, was helping him out. Granny and Wade were sick, and Wayne was a baby. Uncle Oliver was in the kitchen fixing a dose of medicine for the baby. Grandpa called him to bring the lamp. He said, "I think Wade is dying." Granny jumped out of the bed and fainted. She was in bed for six weeks with pneumonia.

Wade did die. That was 1910, and Grandpa died in 1913. While he was sick, his fever went real high. Mama would put washcloths on his face. He would tell her, "You don't need to do that. It will do no good." He told Granny, "Anna, I can't take you with me, but I will take the children." No one ever really knew what he meant. My grandmother lived to be 93 years old. Most of the children died young.

Granny had a hard time after Grandpa died. She had no family here and was not in contact with her family in Alabama. Grandpa had family here, but they didn't help her. She loaned the kids out to work for their upkeep. Mama stayed with Isam and Maggie Trummel. Maggie was in bed with a new baby and Isam Lee was small. Isam would beat him, and Mama couldn't stand that. I don't think she stayed long there. Aunt Lois worked for Jessie and Roy Haynes. Some of the people in the community did help Granny by bringing food.

When Granny was married to Ed Story, she was pregnant with Vernon. This was 1917, the year Mama married but before she married. Mama thought she heard

Earl Stubbs

Ed hit Granny. She picked up a hammer, went in there, and asked, "Did you hit her?"

Ed said, "No."

Granny said, "No."

Later, Granny said he did, but she knew Mama would hit him with that hammer so she said no.

Once when Lawrence was little, he got mad at somebody--I think it was Mama. Lawrence said, "I'm going to sue you."

Mama asked, "How do you sue somebody?"

He said, "Put them in a pen and say, "Suey, Suey."

In the spring of 1939 or 1940, Mama and Tuff walked down to Blue Lake. The mayhaws had fallen and Mama waded out in the water and gathered them up in her dress tail. She carried them home and made jelly out of them. It was mmmmgood.

Sometimes, the cows would eat bitter weeds when they came up in the spring and make the milk taste bitter. We always had plenty of milk to drink and cook with, but it was a pretty hard drink when the cows ate bitter weeds.

Sometime, we would make ice cream in the summer. We didn't have an ice cream freezer. We had milk and eggs, but had to buy the sugar, ice, and salt to salt the ice down. Ice cream was a real treat for us, as we didn't always have money for sugar and ice. We put the ice cream in a gallon syrup bucket and put spoons in the bucket to keep the ice cream scraped off the sides. We set

Compelling Journey

this bucket in a bigger bucket and chipped ice to put in the big bucket around the smaller bucket. Then we would turn the syrup bucket back and forth by the handle until the ice cream was frozen. We probably didn't do this more than four or five times. Maybe not that much, but it was such a treat we will never forget it.

In 1944, Lawrence came home on furlough. He had just finished Navy boot camp in California. He rode the train home, but was sick. He got off the train in Hughes Springs and went to Dr. Jenkins office. Dr. Jenkins asked if he had any folks in town. Eunice and Tom Dudley lived in town and Lawrence went there. Aunt Annie was there with them. Aunt Annie and Eunice thought Lawrence was drunk. Then, they realized he was sick. He probably had a high fever. They put him to bed and got word to Papa. Dr. Jenkins sent Lawrence to Veterans Hospital at Letourneau in Longview. Brother Reeder drove Lawrence and Papa down there. Papa didn't think much of Brother Reeder's driving. He would pass cars on hills and curves. This was in the days of small highways, one lane going each way. Also, there were not many cars on the road. That, and the Good Lord's watchful care, was the reason they safely reached their destination.

Papa had an old car. He carried Tuff and Lavern to see Lawrence while he was in the hospital. They had Lawrence under an oxygen tent, and he seemed to be somewhat asleep. Apparently, he was in pain as he

Earl Stubbs

grunted with every breath. It probably hurt to breath, since he had a bad case of pneumonia. They treated him with sulpha drugs. On the way home, we had car trouble in Ore City. Papa got the car to a garage there, and the mechanic carried us home. We lived at Cornett. He fixed the car and brought it to us in a few days.

Jean, Morris, and JoNell went to see Lawrence. JoNell was in school. Morris and Jean went by the school, and Jean told them she was JoNell's aunt. They got her out of school to go with them. Jean was just barely pregnant with Donnie. When she saw Lawrence and smelled the medicine, she got sick. She went outside and sat down on the steps. Two soldiers saw her and asked if she was sick. She doesn't remember answering them, but then she woke up she was in a bed. She apparently passed out about the time the soldiers asked her if she was sick.

The nurses couldn't get Lawrence to respond to them. They would call him William and he wouldn't answer. Then they would try "Bill" and he still wouldn't answer. Jean told them, "Try calling him Lawrence." When they called him Lawrence, he answered.

During World War II, rationing was common. The folks at home suffered a few hardships, but that was nothing compared with what our troops in the battle suffered. Tires were scarce. Papa had some tires, and he traded them to Carr McKinney for a cow. He named the cow, "Bonnie" after Carr's wife. Papa gave Bonnie to Lawrence. She was a good cow and produced good calves.

Compelling Journey

Lawrence would never sell her. He kept her until she died.

When the family lived close to Herbert Arnold's store at Cornett, Bruce Thomas borrowed some money from Papa. Bruce had a car, but Papa didn't. Mama wanted to go see Aunt Nett. She lived in Avinger, so she got Bruce to take her, Jean, and Lawrence to see Aunt Nett.

Mama always breast fed her babies. When Alvis and Auvis were born, their mouths were too small to nurse. She pumped milk from her breast and fed them with an eyedropper. They did get able to nurse, and she breast-fed them until she died. Afterwards, we fed them with a canned milk formula. They didn't grow much until they were about three months old. Aunt Opal was there with us trying to help with them. She kept changing the formula every day or so. Papa asked Dr. Jenkins about putting them on cow's milk. He told him how to prepare the milk, and when we had some fresh cows (with new calves), Papa put them on cow's milk. We heated the milk to scalding stage on the wood stove, and then when the weather warmed up; we kept it in the icebox. We bought ice to put in the box to keep the icebox cool. The iceman delivered it to the house three times a week. We would get a 50 # block of ice. When Alvis and Auvis started drinking cow's milk, they started growing.

Earl Stubbs

George and Ruth Hampton

18

Assume a virtue, if you have it not--William Shakespeare

GEESE

Robert Marlin Hampton

We had geese on the farm. They were not just for show. They earned their living just like everyone and every other thing on the farm.

We used them to keep the grass out of the cotton fields. Each morning, we drove the geese out into the cotton patch and kept them out there eating grass until the heat of the day. Then, we let them out for the rest of the day.

Also, we picked feathers from the geese. We penned the geese in a stable, and then caught them one at a time. Evelyn and Jean would take a goose, turn it over on its back in their laps, and hold its long neck and head under one arm. Then they would pick the soft downy feathers from the breast and stomach area of the goose.

Earl Stubbs

When they got a handful of feathers, they would put them in a sack so they wouldn't blow away. We made pillows and feather mattresses out of the feathers.

In the late thirties, we lived on the Heard Farm. Someone in Naples contracted with some of the farmers of the area to grow cucumbers for market. Papa decided to plant some. I think about 1 1/2 acres. We kept the vines turned up and down the rows, which made them much easier to pick. We rolled the vines up from one side and picked, and then we rolled the vines up from the other side and picked it. We had to pick them every other day, but I don't recall picking on Sunday. I 'm sure the shed was not open on Sunday, but we never made a habit of working in the field on Sunday. We would start picking early in the morning. After we picked them, someone carried them to Naples. We kids hated this job of picking but we learned to do whatever needed doing. I'm sure this cash crop was lots of help and came at a good time-probably late May and into June and July if the season was right. It wasn't as hard to gather watermelons and besides they were ready to eat and so good.

Compelling Journey

1955
Top Row: Robert, Lawrence, Morris, Auvis, George Weldon, and Alvis
Bottom Row: Annie, Lavern, George, Ima Jean, and Evelyn

19

MEMORIES

Annie Orlean Hampton Crossland

I was nineteen months older than Morris. I remember watching after him and keeping him pulled back on the quilt while Mamma hoed nut grass out of the Cotton. He was probably five or six-months-old which made me two-years-old or a little older

Our house, that papa built down what we called the old place, had a crack in the floor between the two rooms. Papa probably did not have a plank left to make a piece to cover the crack. Morris was a crawling baby, and when he found anything that would go through that crack, he put it through, like combs and Mamma's thimble. Mamma would tell me to crawl down under the doorsteps and go under the house to get her thimble.

Mr. Ben Taylor lived across Tar Kill Creek, and he had a bull that stayed out of the pasture more than it stayed in. When the bull was in our yard, Mama had to do a lot of coaxing to get me to go under the house.

Compelling Journey

One day when Mama was in the bed when Evelyn was born, that old ugly bull came up to the window and balled real loud. Morris and I ran and got in the bed with Mama.

Morris, Evelyn, Lawrence, Alvis, Auvis, and I were born in that old bungalow house. There was a house there before Papa built the bungalow. I don't know if I was born in that house. I remember they left a room of the old house, and we used it for a smoke house. One day Mama was doctoring a sick chicken. She had a little kerosene in a jar lid. Evelyn picked up the lid and drank the kerosene. There wasn't enough to make her sick, but it frightened Mama.

I don't remember when Evelyn was born, but when Lawrence came 6 December, it must have been a warm day. I know Aunt Net, Irene, and Mayo were there. We children slept on a pallet made of quilts in the other bedroom.

I woke up, and Aunt Net came in to get us settled down to sleep.

Ima Jean was born at Cornett, but I don't remember where we stayed. Dr. Harry Haynes delivered all of us through Ima Jean. He was the son of Elijah Haynes. They ran a store at Cornett. Harry married Nora Stroman, sister of Arthur Stroman. Harry and Nora had two girls—one named Arlene. The Haynes family moved west for the Dr.'s health.

Earl Stubbs

Dr. Jenkins of Hughes Springs delivered the rest of the children.

When George Weldon was born at Cornett, Cousin Minnie Hampton's boys came to spend the night, as mamma went into labor. Papa got Mr. Herbert Arnold to carry Cousin Minnie's boys and our boys back to Cousin Minnie's house. She apologized. I spent the night with Faye Betts. Faye and I slept with Bernie and Myra.

When one phone rang, all the phones in the community rang. When the phone rang, Myra slipped out of bed to eavesdrop. She came back and told us papa had called the doctor. After a while, the phone rang again. Myra went to eavesdrop. She came back and said Annie has a baby brother. I felt relieved that Mama and the baby were okay.

When Lavern was born, I spent the night with Joyce Gibson. When I came home, they told me I had a baby sister. She was born at Cornett.

When Tuff was born, I spent the night with Aunt Alma.

I think we kept Lavern. Aunt Sallie kept some of the children. Tuff was born on what we called the Heard place, because a merchant and cotton buyer named Milton N. Heard owned it. He bought the land from Moody Cotton Company.

Robert Marlin (Tuff) was born before midnight on 15 January and Robert Earl was born after midnight 16

Compelling Journey

January. Mamma's sister, Gertrude, begged mama to name Tuff Robert Earl.

Tuffy would fall down, but he wouldn't cry. That's how he got his nickname. He just got up and tried again. Riley Gibson called him Tuffy.

Papa went to Fayetteville Arkansas, to the V.A. hospital when Tuff was a crawling baby. Morris and I stayed home from school to help Mama. She and Morris worked the crop, and I cared for Lavern and Tuff and worked at the house.

One day, Lavern and Tuff were playing under the front porch in the dirt. Lavern came in the house and told me Tuff had crawled way up under the house. He had gotten up to where the house was low on the ground. I crawled as far as I could and began to talk him back to me. When he would start back he would bump his head on the floor joist, and he would stop and cry. He finally got to where I could reach him, and I pulled him out.

When Alvis and Auvis were born, I was 22 years old. Lawrence came after me. Albert and I lived at Cornett on Mildred and Marion's place. Mama and Papa lived on the old place at Crossroads. Papa got up early to carry a bale of cotton to Hughes Springs to the cotton gin. Leona Hall carried Albert to take the cotton on to the gin and brought Papa home. Ima Jean missed school and took care of Carlton Ray. I think Lawrence went to school. Alvis arrived into this world just as Papa got home. He was so tiny. I didn't understand until Dr. Jenkins said it

Earl Stubbs

was a breech. I didn't really know what he meant. This was the first we knew there were twins. The birth of Auvis caused a bruise on one of his arms, and he groaned like an adult, but he finally quit that.

When the small children would miss behave I told them I could see them, because I had eyes in the back of my head. One day I was sewing on the machine when Alvis did something, and I said something to him about it. He came around behind me looking and said, "Annie have you all really got eyes in the back of your head?"

Compelling Journey

20

God bless thee; and put meekness in thy mind, love, charity, obedience, and true duty!--William Shakespeare

Evelyn's Stories

Mama's Flowers

Mama always loved flowers and worked hard to have something growing in the yard. When we lived at Cornett, east of the store, our house was in the pasture, but we had a picket fence around the front yard. She had moss rose, petunias, zinnias, marigolds, blanket flowers, and bachelor buttons. Lavern was born December 26, 1931, and Mama had a rose bush in bloom.

In the spring and summer of 1940, she had a flower garden between the house and road. Papa plowed the spot and made several rows that she planted mostly with zinnias. We have a picture of Mama standing in them. The flowers reached higher than her waist. Good food for the soul.

Earl Stubbs

The Cucumber Patch

In the late 1930's, Papa began growing cucumbers for the market. It was an early cash crop that met a need. I think he planted about two acres. We trained the vines to run up and down the row, which made them easier to pick, and we could plow the middle to control the grass and weeds. The best size was four to five inches long, which brought the best price. They took larger sizes but didn't pay as much per pound for them. We picked them every other day. I don't recall that we ever picked on Sunday. After we picked them, someone had to carry them to market in Marietta, Naples, or Hughes Springs--a trip of about 6-10 miles one way. George Weldon remembered one time we picked them, and our old pick up would not start. He and Lawrence carried them to Hughes Springs in the wagon. He recalled that they brought less than three dollars. Of course, this would have been in the early 1940's. We all hated to gather this crop, but I'm sure it was a great help to our parents, and it kept us kids out of meanness.

Christmas at Our House

Christmas was always a joyful time at our home. Mama and Papa saw to that. There was great excitement getting ready. We cleaned the yards. We raked, swept,

Compelling Journey

and burned the trash. We made the brush brooms used to sweep the yard out of small dogwood trees tied together with strings. If the smoke was white then you had been good, and Santa would come to see you. If the smoke was dark, you were going to get a sack of switches and ashes. I don't remember that we ever did.

Our Christmas tree was always special to us. We cut a fresh one and decorated with whatever we had such as stringed popped corn, etc. One year at Cornett, east of the store, we had a tree so large it touched the ceiling (probably 10-12ft. ceilings) and covered most of the large room. We decorated it with red and green roping and balloons.

Santa always came, and whichever child woke first, the others soon followed. Then Papa got up and built a fire to keep us warm. I remember one year, after Annie and Albert were married, Mama and Papa made Lavern some doll furniture. There was a doll bed with a mattress, a dresser with a mirror, table and two chairs (one chair for Tuff) all painted blue. Lavern wouldn't you like to have that today, but you really enjoyed it then. George Weldon got a red goat cart. We had a pet goat at that time, and we hitched him to the cart quite often.

Each child always got an apple, orange, candy, and nuts along with a toy. We all shared the games. A little red "Radio Flyer" wagon was a family gift to share. The last gift I remember getting from Santa was a little Cedar

Earl Stubbs

Chest with stationary in it. I probably was fourteen or fifteen years old. I still have the little chest today in 2003.

We always had plenty of good food. Chicken and dressing was a favorite and still is with the descendants. One other thing I vividly remember was the orange cake Mama made. She made her regular cake that she baked in layers in the oven of the wood stove. How did she set the temperature? She made a boiled icing (we called it seven-minute frosting) to stack the cake and put thin slices of oranges between the layers and on top. After it set a few days, it was delicious. She also made a good jam cake with homemade berry jam.

Compelling Journey

Anna Liza Herren Hampton
Age 94

Earl Stubbs

21

Descendant Report for William Henry Hampton

..... 1 William Henry Hampton b: 17 Feb 1877 in Talladega County, Alabama, USA, d: 28 Nov 1912 in Omaha, Morris County, Texas, USA
..... + Anna Liza Herren b: 05 Dec 1880 in Alabama Clay County, m: Oct 1894 in Talladega, Alabama, USA, d: 16 Dec 1973 in Morris County, USA
.... 2 Mattie Odessa Hampton b: 1895 in Alabama, USA, d: 1895 in Alabama, USA
.... 2 Zeala B Hampton b: Dec 1897 in Alabama, d: Sep 1915 in Texas
.... 2 Zelma Ruth Hampton b: 26 May 1898, d: 25 Nov 1940 in Morris, Texas, United States
།།།།།།།།།། + George Hampton m: 16 Dec 1917 in Morris County, Texas
.... 3 Annie Orlean Hampton b: 19 Oct 1918
.... + Albert Harry Crossland b: 28 Jan 1917, m: 15 Feb 1936
.... 4 Carlton Ray Crossland b: 20 Jul 1939

Compelling Journey

.... + Carol Ann Odell m: 20 Apr 1963
.... 5 Jonetta Kay Crossland b: 15 Oct 1961
.... 6 Anthony Carlos Acevedo b: 31 Jan 1988
.... + Era Anne McKiney b: 20 Nov 1944
.... 4 Ruth Ann Crossland b: 23 Sep 1942
.... + Michael Vann Pepper b: 25 Sep 1939, d: 03 Apr 1975
.... 5 Mark Alton Pepper b: 22 Feb 1962
.... + Rhonda Lynn Stark m: 05 Jan 1979
.... 6 MIchael Van Pepper Jr. b: 20 May 1981
.... + Denise Torres Thompkins
.... 6 Tahnee Nicole Pepper b: 20 Mar 1986
.... 5 Vanessa Ruth Pepper b: 01 Aug 1965
.... 6 Dustin Jacob Pepper b: 14 Aug 1983
.... 6 Paul Michael Pepper b: 23 Jan 1986
.... + Tony Creic Carr b: 26 Feb 1963

Earl Stubbs

.... 6 Brianna Cheree Carr b: 25 Apr 1989
.... 6 Ashley Shenea Carr b: 14 Mar 1991
.... 3 Morris Paul Hampton b: 20 May 1920
.... + Hadee Golden b: 07 Sep 1922
.... 4 Barbara Gail Hampton b: 22 Jun 1942
.... + Charles Irvin m: 23 Jun 1978
.... 5 Charles David Irvin b: 09 Feb 1959
.... + Pandora Lee Goswich b: 10 Sep 1956, m: 14 Jan 1978
.... 6 Claleigh Jenea Irvin b: 03 Jun 1979
.... 6 Colton Irvin b: 22 Mar 1988
.... 5 Sandra Kay Irvin b: 21 Feb 1960
.... + Larry Avery Goswick b: 22 Jun 1958, m: 04 Apr 1978
.... 6 Brandon Avery Goswick b: 06 Mar 1981
.... 6 Shane Ross Goswick b: 25 Mar 1983
.... 5 James Ray Irvin b: 22 Sep 1962

Compelling Journey

.... + Teresa DiAnn Pryor b: 07 May 1962, m: 10 Apr 1983
.... 5 Stacy Jo Irvin b: 10 Sep 1967
.... + Curtis Brice b: 09 Jan 1961, m: 21 Jun 1986
.... 6 Jordan Brice b: 23 Jun 1988
.... + Donald Ray Sharbono m: 23 Jun 1978
.... 5 Donna Lorraine Sharbono b: 27 Oct 1964
.... + John Gregory Atkinson b: 10 Dec 1956, m: 22 Oct 1982
.... 6 John Christopher Atkinson b: 12 Jun 1984
.... 6 Daniel Aaron Atkinson b: 17 Jan 1987
.... 4 Gerald Elwyn Hampton b: 05 Dec 1944
.... + Bessie Yevonne Hensley b: 12 Oct 1945, m: 07 Sep 1963
.... 5 Scott Anthony Hampton b: 30 Sep 1967
.... + Laura Lee Talbot b: 22 Feb 1967
.... 6 Justin Cole Hampton b: 23 Jan 1992

Earl Stubbs

.... 6   Jessica Brooke Hampton b: 25 Jan 1995
.... 6   Jenna Alyse Hampton b: 17 Nov 1998
.... 5   Sheri Renee Hampton b: 29 Nov 1970
....   + Brent Easley b: 15 Dec 1967
....   + Wade James Cobb b: 02 Feb 1958, m: 20 Apr 1996
.... 6   Tyler Wade Cobb b: 19 Sep 1999
.... 6   Tanner Gerald Cobb b: 02 Feb 2000
.... 5   Robert Charles Hampton b: 21 Feb 1976
....   + Carrie Lee Ritchie b: 14 Aug 1975, m: 31 Dec 1994
.... 6   Faith Nicole Hampton b: 26 Sep 2002
.... 5   Jeremy Roy Hampton b: 15 Mar 1978
.... 4   Gary Paul Hampton b: 29 Jan 1948
....   + Charlotte Hall b: 11 Jan 1949
.... 5   Christy Michelle Hampton b: 01 Oct 1969
.... 5   Brian Allen Hampton b: 28 Jul 1973

Compelling Journey

.... 4 Tommie Lynn Hampton b: 03 Jul 1949
.... + Bonnie Alford b: 05 Aug 1953
.... 5 Wendy Hampton b: 27 Sep 1974
.... 4 Carolyn Sue Hampton b: 19 Oct 1951
.... + Charles Richard Turner b: 06 Apr 1945, m: 12 Nov 1970
.... 5 Aaron Paul Turner b: 01 May 1974
.... 5 Darren Matthew Turner b: 01 Jun 1977
.... 4 Ronald Hampton b: 18 Jun 1954
.... + Susan Alice Miller b: 05 Apr 1949, m: 23 Mar 1983
.... 4 Kenneth Dewayne Hampton b: 03 Nov 1955
.... + Mona Lee Powell b: 02 Mar 1957, m: 26 Aug 1973
.... 5 Christopher Dewayne Hampton b: 12 Dec 1974
.... 5 Jennifer Lee Hampton b: 12 Nov 1976
.... 5 Joshua Travis Hampton b: 19 Apr 1984

.... 5   Nathan Ryan Hampton b: 30 Jun 1986
.... 4   Kevin Ray Hampton b: 02 Dec 1964
....   + Susan Celeste Bishop b: 13 Sep 1962
.... 5   Nicholas Ryan Hampton b: 24 Mar 1985
.... 5   Charles Mark Hampton b: 12 Aug 1980
.... 3   Edna Evelyn Hampton b: 15 Mar 1922 in Cass County, Texas, USA
....   + James Leonard Jacobs b: 22 Apr 1921, m: 20 Jun 1942
.... 4   James Douglas Jacobs b: 17 Aug 1943
....   + Demeris Ann Downs b: 02 Sep 1946, m: 02 Sep 1963
.... 5   Darryl Allen Jacobs b: 31 May 1964
....   + Suanna Waldrop b: 19 Nov 1963, m: 28 Sep 1984
.... 5   James Darren Jacobs b: 06 Aug 1966
....   + Meloni Huffman b: 14 Jan 1969, m: 16 May 1987
.... 6   Matthew Thomas Jacobs b: 22 Jun 1988

Compelling Journey

.... 5 Jessica Darlene Jacobs
.... 4 Marilyn Ruth Jacobs b: 07 Nov 1954
.... + Timothy Smith m: 17 Aug 1973
.... 5 Kendra Michelle Smith b: 21 Jun 1979
.... 3 William Lawrence Hampton b: 06 Dec 1923
.... + Jo Nell Dennis b: 30 Apr 1929, m: 17 Aug 1946
.... 4 Brenda Joyce Hampton b: 15 Sep 1947
.... + John Adams m: 05 Apr 1974
.... 5 Matt Thomas Adams b: 21 Jul 1970
.... 5 Melodie Lynn Adams b: 13 Jun 1972
.... + Willie Dean Godwin m: 04 Sep 1943
.... 5 Deidre Godwin b: 09 Jun 1965
.... 5 Kendra Godwin b: 07 Apr 1972
.... 4 Rhonda Kay Hampton b: 13 Feb 1956
.... + Mack Skipper m: 03 Mar 1983
.... 5 William Jamerson Scott Skipper b: 08 Feb 1974
.... + Louis W. Pitts b: 03 Aug 1956

Earl Stubbs

.... 5   Kristen Marnell Pitts b: 16 Jul 1984
.... 5   Karen Marie Pitts b: 10 May 1987

.... 3   Zelma Ima Jean Hampton b: 02 Oct 1925
....   + Mannie X. Davis b: 22 Jun 1924, m: 25 Dec 1943
.... 4   Mannie Don Davis b: 12 Aug 1945
....   + Bonnie Pilkington
.... 5   James Michael Davis b: 08 Sep 1956
.... 5   Donald Ray Davis b: 14 Oct 1967
.... 5   Jerry Lynn Davis b: 04 Nov 1971
.... 5   Jeffrey Wayne Davis b: 25 Feb 1976
.... 4   Glinda Ruth Davis b: 07 Nov 1947
....   + Lonnie Farmer b: 24 Oct 1944, m: 14 Jun 1968, d: 2003
.... 5   Lisa Michelle Farmer b: 16 Oct 1971
....   + Rodney Goodman b: 1962
.... 6   Jesse Goodman b: 2003
.... 4   Bobbie Jean Davis b: 25 Oct 1949
....   + James Oliver Simmons

Compelling Journey

.... 5 Chad Lamar Simmons b: 21 Apr 1971
.... 5 Jeremy Simmons b: 31 Dec 1973, d: 26 Apr 1974
.... + Jackie Yee b: 21 Sep 1944
.... 5 Mark Yee b: 16 Nov 1969
.... 4 Kathy Davis b: 22 Jul 1954
.... + Gary Shoemaker m: 03 Aug 1973
.... 5 Aaron Shoemaker b: 17 Jul 1978
.... 5 Adam Shoemaker b: 03 Aug 1982
.... + Karl Loritsch
.... 5 Lydia Loritsch
.... 5 Mika Loritsch
.... 3 George Weldon Hampton b: 14 Sep 1929
.... + Pansy Armstrong
.... 4 James Weldon Hampton b: 19 Mar 1955
.... + Cynthia Anne Keiller b: 15 Mar 1954, m: 03 Mar 1979
.... 5 Darcy Ann Hampton b: 28 Jan 1980
.... 5 Austin Keiller Hampton b: 06 Apr 1983
.... 5 Travis George Hampton b: 08 Dec 1984

Earl Stubbs

.... 5 Samuel Weldon Hampton b: 22 May 1989
.... 4 Michael Anthony Hampton b: 29 Aug 1958
.... + Sharon Louise Putman b: 20 Jan 1957, m: 12 Nov 1983
.... 5 Jenna Renee Hampton b: 30 Jan 1985
.... 5 Jarrod Hampton b: 24 Jan 1989
.... + Margie Welborn
.... 4 Mike Welborn b: 14 Jun 1958
.... + Elizabeth McKinney b: 24 Feb 1964, m: 25 May 1958
.... 4 Anna Welborn b: 15 Feb 1965
.... + Jeffery Clubb m: 19 Jul 1986
.... 3 Alma Lavern Hampton b: 26 Dec 1931
.... + Horace Thomas Vaughan b: 19 Sep 1931, m: 03 Jun 1950
.... 4 Thomas Wade Vaughan b: 10 Jun 1955
.... + Jacqueline Marie Kennedy b: 26 Jan 1957, m: 22 Sep 1978
.... 5 Zachery Thomas Vaughan b: 08 Oct 1982
.... 5 Kimberly Diane Vaughan b: 12 Jan 1985

Compelling Journey

.... 5 Daniel Wade Vaughan b: 30 Oct 1988
.... 4 David Wayne Vaughan b: 14 May 1956
.... 4 Roger Ennis Vaughan b: 02 May 1960
.... + Rhonda Beaver b: 12 Feb 1962, m: 01 Nov 1980
.... 5 Lacee Annette Vaughan b: 06 Dec 1982
.... 5 Katie Lynnette Vaughan b: 23 Sep 1985
.... 3 Robert Marlin Hampton b: 15 Jan 1934
.... + Mary Armstrong m: 13 Jan 1979
.... 4 Julia Ann Hampton b: 03 Mar 1958
.... 4 Lynn Hampton Beck b: 13 Mar 1959
.... + Cynthia Laney
.... 4 John Maxie Laney b: 01 Mar 1961
.... + Laura Lee Richey m: 06 Feb 1988
.... 4 Jeffery Carrol Laney b: 26 Mar 1962
.... + Melissa Diane Hawkins m: 10 Oct 1987
.... 3 Alvis Wade Hampton b: 22 Oct 1940

~ 149 ~

Earl Stubbs

.... + Bennie Alexander b: 24 Jan 1946, m: 04 Aug 1980
.... 4   Justin Wade Hampton b: 11 Apr 1982
.... 4   Kevin Don Alexander b: 18 May 1973
.... 4   Anita Darlene Alexander b: 19 Mar 1968
....   + James Bagley b: 07 Oct 1965, m: Apr 1986
.... 5   Joshua Allen Bagley b: 09 Oct 1987
.... 3   Auvis Wayne Hampton b: 22 Oct 1940
....   + Lola Jean Vaught b: 12 May 1944, m: 15 Nov 1969
.... 4   Steven Lance Hampton b: 12 Jan 1974
.... 4   Spencer Landon Hampton b: 11 Mar 1976
.... 2   Nettie Gaye Hampton b: 12 Oct 1900 in Alabama, d: 03 Apr 1933 in Texas, United States
....   + Charlie Lou McMichael b: 07 Feb 1892, m: Oct 1917, d: 30 Dec 1969 in Texarkana, Bowie, Texas, United States of America
.... 3   Ludine McMichael b: 1918, d: 1918
.... 3   Alice Irine McMichael b: 03 Sep 1920
.... 4   Betty Ruth Westmoreland b: 24 Dec 1939

Compelling Journey

.... + James David Gimlin b: 25 Apr 1939, m: 04 Sep 1958
.... 5 Lisa Kimberly Gimlin b: 23 May 1959
.... + Danny Barabas m: 27 Dec
.... 6 Bradley David Barabas b: 30 Jan 1985
.... 5 Kelly Michelle Gimlin b: 26 Feb 1968
.... 4 Jo Ann Westmoreland b: 06 Nov 1941
.... + Winfred Earl Shaw
.... 5 Winfred Earl (Shaw) Luscomb b: 03 Sep 1960
.... + Mary Smith
.... 6 Barbara Rosa Luscomb
.... 5 James Kenneth (Shaw) Luscomb b: 25 Dec 1961
.... 5 Barbara Jo Ann (Shaw) Luscomb b: 1962
.... + Bobby McKensley
.... 6 James Brandon Luscomb
.... 6 Justin
.... + Bill Luscomb
.... 5 Judy Price Luscomb b: 05 May 1965
.... 4 Mary Alice Westmoreland b: 25 Jun 1944

Earl Stubbs

.... + Robert J. Polk
.... 5 James Randall Westmoreland b: 07 Apr 1964
.... 5 Robert Kevin Polk b: 25 Aug 1968
.... 4 James Author Westmoreland b: 05 Dec 1947
.... + Brenda Sue Stephens
.... 5 Tammy Renes Westmoreland b: 16 Jan 1968
.... + Ricky
.... 5 Jamey Westmoreland b: 22 May 1976
.... + Donna Johnson
.... 6 Amy Johnson
.... 5 Richard Wayne Westmoreland b: 26 May 1983
.... 4 Linda Mayo Westmoreland b: 13 Jun 1949
.... + James Marvin Ward m: 06 Jun 1966
.... 5 Tracey Lynn Ward b: 26 Dec 1969
.... 5 Terry Marvin Ward b: 13 Jul 1973
.... 4 Ennis Michael Westmoreland b: 09 Mar 1957

Compelling Journey

.... 3 William Mayo McMichael b: 30 Mar 1922
.... + Margret
.... 4 Herman Wayne McMichael b: 13 Apr 1944
.... + Ruth Ann
.... 5 Gina Kay McMichael b: 01 Apr
.... 5 Dan McMichael b: 05 Feb
.... + Betty Jo Fisher b: 23 Mar 1922, d: 23 Jun 1972
.... 3 Juliette McMichael b: Dec 1926
.... + C L McMichael m: Oct 1917
.... 2 Alma Lois Hampton b: Aug 1903 in Alabama, d: 01 Jan 1936 in Texas, United States
.... + Clurn Gibson b: Abt. 1903
.... 2 Willie Gertrude Hampton b: 15 Oct 1905 in Lineville, Alabama, d: 09 Jul 1936 in Texarkana, Miller, Arkansas, United States
.... + Marvin Lester Stubbs b: 03 Sep 1900 in Cass County Texas, d: 01 Jan 1976 in Morris County Texas
.... 3 Anna Marvalyn Stubbs b: 12 Mar 1925 in Cass County Texas
.... + Blewett Garland Cotton b: 24 Dec 1917 in Blossom, Lamar, Texas, USA, m: 30 Jun 1949 in Avery, Red River, Texas, USA, d: 21 Sep 1962 in Kansas
.... 4 Carol Lynn Cotton b: 26 Apr 1953 in Clarksville, TX

Earl Stubbs

.... + Gregory Charles Shirley b: 10 Sep 1952, m: 07 Jun 1980 in Albuquerque, NM
.... 5   Justin Scott Shirley b: 23 Dec 1977
.... 5   Allison Leigh Shirley b: 23 Sep 1980
.... 4   Gary Blewett Cotton b: 14 Jun 1958
.... + Cindy Kay Oliver b: 23 May 1960
.... 5   Phillip Ryan Cotton b: 07 Aug 1985
.... 5   Stephen Mark Cotton b: 13 Apr 1988
.... 3   Dorothy Jean Stubbs b: 02 Apr 1930
.... + Joe Tom Terrell m: 08 Nov 1952
.... 4   Tommy Jack Terrell b: 01 Oct 1954, d: 1994 in Winnsboro, TX
.... + Terri Lynn Garren b: 27 Apr 1955
.... 5   Thomas Joe Terrell b: 1987
.... 5   Trenton Billy Terrell b: 1990
.... 3   Earl Wayne Stubbs b: 10 Aug 1934 in Marietta, Cass, Texas, USA
.... + Nancy Lynn Jacobs b: 03 Feb 1937, m: 31 Jul 1954 in Farmersville, TX
.... 4   Michael Wayne Stubbs b: 17 Jun 1957 in Greenville, Texas
.... + Cincy Louise Near b: 17 Sep 1961, m: 11 Jul 1981 in Dallas, Texas, USA

Compelling Journey

.... 5 Travis Wayne Stubbs b: 11 Mar 1987 in Dallas, Texas, USA
.... 5 Jordan William Stubbs b: 16 Aug 1991 in Dallas, Texas, USA
.... 4 Mark Allen Stubbs b: 31 Aug 1960 in Greenville, Texas
.... + Carolyn Cougar b: 29 Dec 1961, m: 08 Aug 198
.... 5 Jennifer Ellen Stubbs b: 16 Feb 1995 in Witchita Falls, Texas
.... 5 Kayla Lynn Stubbs b: 16 Feb 1995 in Witchita Falls, Texas
.... 5 Aaron Mark Stubbs b: 15 Nov 1996
.... 2 Wade Hampton b: 1908 in Alabama, d: 1910 in Naples, Morris County, Texas
.... 2 Alonzo Wayne Hampton b: 14 Aug 1909 in Texas, d: 14 Jul 1974 in Linden, Cass, Texas, United States
.... + Velma Howell
.... 3 Joseph Henry Hampton b: 07 Nov 1937
.... + Majorie Alford b: 28 Oct, m: 27 Dec 1963
.... 3 Floyd Wayne Hampton b: 22 Dec 1939
.... + Patricia Welchel m: 22 Feb 1961
.... 4 Anthony Wayne Hampton b: 24 Jan 1962

~ 155 ~

Earl Stubbs

.... + Rebecca Ann Moss
.... 5 Holly Lou Ann Hampton b: 1985
.... 5 Jasmine Hampton b: 1988
.... + Cynthia Ann Brailean
.... 4 Kaylean Elizabeth Hampton b: 27 Feb 1973
.... 3 Robert Dan Hampton b: 17 Sep 1942
.... + Ann Rowley
.... 4 Robert Wade Hampton b: 24 Sep 1971
.... + Patty
4   Lucy Angelia Hampton b: 22 Aug 1953
+ Jimmy Howard Pogue b: 04 Oct 1953, m: 04 Oct 1970
.... 4 Kelly Angelia Pogue b: 1971
.... + Baumeister
.... 5 Trenton Shane Baumeister b: 1993
.... 5 Allyssa Ann Baumeister b: 1994
.... + Vernon
.... 5 Joshua Philip Vernon b: 25 Aug 2000
.... 5 Mathew Bradie Vernon b: 25 Aug 2000
.... 4 Jamie Kathlene Pogue b: 1973
.... 4 Leslie Nicole Pogue b: 1982

Compelling Journey

.... + Scantling
.... 5 Oubree Nicole Scantling b: 1997
.... 2 Pansy Opal Hampton b: 30 Mar 1911, d: 04 Sep 1989 in Maud, Bowie, Texas, United States
.... + Leon B. Hitt b: 12 Aug 1916, m: 04 Nov 1957

Earl Stubbs

Book III

22

I never did give anybody hell. I just told the truth and they thought it was hell—Harry S. Truman

AUTOBIOGRAPHY

I arrived August 10, 1934, in the Flat Creek community of Cass County, Texas, as the third and last child of Marvin and Gertrude Stubbs. Our mother passed in July of 1936 leaving my sisters and me without a home. My father, Marvin, had a crop to harvest, so he farmed us out to anyone who would take us.

My earliest recollections are of an old white house nestled about twenty yards from the Cotton Belt railroad near the town square in Mt. Pleasant, Texas. That was during the rail age, and those old steam engines rumbled past our house twenty-four hours each day making thunderous sounds, spewing steam, and smelling of oil.

I lived with my aunt, Ella Clyde Stubbs Price, her daughter, Ella Mae Price Barker, and her husband, John L. Barker. John worked as a plumber. Ella Clyde's

Compelling Journey

husband Judson Dudley Price, worked on the Sulfur River as a bridge watchman. He was rarely home.

ELLA CLYDE STUBBS PRICE

Aside from the normal activities of bouncing an old tennis ball off the chimney, using the front porch swing as my own personal locomotive, and building dirt roads for my toy cars, I joined my family making periodic trips of about thirty miles to the old home place in the Flat Creek Community of Cass County. We drove from Mt. Pleasant to Flat Creek in our black, 1937 Plymouth sedan, which was one of the few cars in the entire family.

The last five or so miles past Marietta, the dirt roads, bumpy with deep ruts, made riding down the hilly road quite an adventure. The ride ended in a visit with Grandpa Jim Stubbs, my father, Marvin, and any other member of the family who might drop in on a warm Sunday.

Earl Stubbs

Grandpa James Madison Stubbs was the patriarch of the Cass County Stubbs clan. He was a small wiry man generally respected if not feared due to a hair-trigger temper and a handy weapon--a reputation I suspect he cultivated since he was more bluster than substance. He would fight at the drop of a hat, often carried a pistol, and a sharp pocketknife. He reflected energy, dipped snuff, and had beard stubble that he loved to rub on my tender face.

Lucy Ivy Stubbs, Grandpa's first wife and our grandmother, passed on before I was born. From listening to conversations between her daughters, Ella Clyde and Aunt Valary, she was an oppressed soul. Nonetheless, Jim and Lucy produced nine children including Valary, Walter, Ella, John, Carl, Liller, Altha Mary, Edgar, and Marvin. John died after nineteen months. Liller at the age of six years, and Altha Mary at the age of eight. Edgar was a severe epileptic and mentally challenged. My father, Marvin, was the youngest child, and as I am the youngest of his family, some of my recollections derive from the recollections of a youngster, hence, they may not be historical fact. However, most of this information will stand up to scrutiny.

I grew up in poor, but not destitute, circumstances. Ella Clyde's husband, Judson Dudley Price, had a real job that paid hard money. He worked for the Cotton Belt Railroad as a Sulphur River bridge watchman, and he lived on the river. His family lived wherever Ella Clyde chose to live. We had some money, but we didn't spend very much of it. The depression taught my family a tough lesson--money in the bank was of far greater importance than the outward show of affluence. We rented.

JUDSON DUDLEY PRICE

It was unfortunate that Ella Clyde's daughter, Ella Mae, could sew, because she felt compelled to make shirts for me to wear to school. She most often made them from flour sacks, and the print design was not always entirely masculine. I wore overalls, long drawers, and high top shoes in winter. We had no indoor plumbing until I was twelve, but I won't elaborate.

I was six by the time we moved to Naples, about eighteen miles east of Mt. Pleasant. Naples was a small town where folks paid little attention to youngsters. Like the dogs that roamed the streets, we were just there. We fended for ourselves and became adept at entertaining ourselves with football, basketball, softball, fox and hound, touching street signs, listening to the radio, reading, riding bicycles, and getting into minor mischief. The center of our entertainment world was the Inez Theater where we saw so many of the wonderful films of the day and the Saturday westerns.

Sports dominated my high school years. I played point guard on three basketball teams and served as captain my junior year. Ankle problems plagued my final year, and I finished the year on the bench. While playing in a PE class my sophomore year at Kilgore Junior College, Coach Turner offered me a scholarship. Since I was already a sophomore, I declined.

I played in the infield in baseball for three years. I made one error, but was not a consistant hitter.

We had three track teams while I was at Pewett. My coach asked me to join Waylon Buchannon in training for the season my sophomore year, but my smoking made the cross country pure agony. I dropped out. The next year I was the district leader in points for sprinting. I set the school record in the process which lasted for several years.

Ankle problems curtailed my football career as well. It is ironic that ankle surgery continues to plague my life as I write this book. When healthy, I could run, pass, and punt to the extent that Catfish Smith of ET offered me a

Compelling Journey

full scholarship. Due to my history of injuries and addiction to cigarettes, I declined. I regret that decision.

After high school, I enrolled at East Texas State Teachers College. My undergraduate college grades fluctuated from dean's list to scholastic probation, but I had a hell of a time. I view those years with trepidation, as I was unable to focus on my reason for being there. However, my social development may have served me well during the ensuing years.

I discovered in graduate school at North Texas State University that if I did my best, my grades markedly improved, and my professors liked me better. I overcame my early environment, grew as a person, and developed tools that became the backbone of a career and a life. I still believe that human relations, reading, simple arithmetic, typing, and public speaking are about the only things I learned in school that were useful in life.

During my first year in college, I roomed with Bill Jacobs from Farmersville, Texas. During a weekend visit to his home, I met his sister, Nancy. Eventually, we married. As of 2012, our union spans almost fifty-eight years.

My work life varied. Michael, our firstborn, arrived two weeks after I graduated from college, so I took the first job offered. It was repossessing cars for a finance company. During the next two and one-half years, management with The Associates Investment Company hired me in Dallas, transferred me to Corpus Christi for training, moved me to Beaumont, and finally, to Houston—all within two years.

Why so much moving around? We Stubbs' are not all blessed with great political skills. That is why many of my predecessors owned farms and ran country stores so they could work for themselves. I did not leave a trail of fans everywhere I worked. My production was always superior so The Associates didn't fire me. They resolved my "charm" issues with a transfer. I had a low tolerance for incompetence and was too immature to realize that the working world is rife with ineffectual people, especially supervisors.

Unwilling to let me repossess his transportation, the last in a series of irate car owners waved his gun in my face, which prompted a career change. I decided the classroom might be a wiser venue for my skills. I became a science teacher in a large Dallas area school system. At first, the classroom was great. The kids loved me and I them. To supplement my income, I worked concession stands at ball games, drove a school bus, tutored, ran a swimming pool in the summer, and taught summer school. After seven years, I used up my last ounce of enthusiasm. Having prepared lesson plans year after year, I lost interest in the subject matter. I was not destined to be a thirty-year man in any field.

About that time, my youngest son, Mark, decided he didn't like daycare. He left school early one day and walked five miles down a busy freeway to come home. He

Compelling Journey

had just turned six. After calling the police, we found him playing in the neighborhood. At that moment, we decided that Nancy needed to stay home from work. That wouldn't happen unless I got out of the teaching profession and into a more lucrative career.

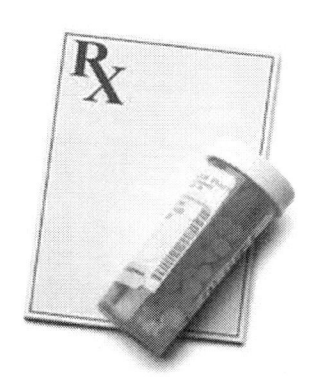

An opportunity to sell pharmaceutical drugs fortuitously presented itself. Nancy's boss, Norman Shipley, was an avid golfer. He routinely played with Harold Walton, the regional manager of a national pharmaceutical company. One fateful day, they put their heads together and came up with me as a candidate for a job opening in Walt's company. I interviewed and got the job. I spent the next seven years with Eaton Labs.

I eventually decided that Southerners did not get promoted in this New York company, so I hooked on with a British pharmaceutical company that had only been in the USA for a year. The company had a great product but lousy management along with a new and untried sales force. I saw opportunity.

In 1979 a new president named Steve arrived from England. He was a man in his twenties. By that time I was in my middle forties. He came to Dallas to work with me since he heard I was the best. After the day in the field, he told me that he was not happy with my work and that I was the worst rep he had ever seen. I was taken aback and peered at him askance.

After reviewing the situation, it occurred to me that the training and information I was getting from the home office was not the best. My answer to this deficit was to head to the medical school library and start researching the realities of my product and the diseases it treated. It took about two days for me to discover how far off base the marketing department of my company and I really were. I copied a paragraph written by Dr. Frank Austen from Harvard Medical School onto my pad and took it home to type it out. I used this paragraph for the next year on all my calls and quickly became the top rep in the company. Steve decided that I knew what I was doing and promoted me to Denver, replacing two reps, where the territory went from last in the company to first in six months. After less than a year, I was given the Southeastern Region and transferred to Memphis. The Southeast region was at the bottom of the national sales

Compelling Journey

barrel. I brought the reps in, taught them my system, and the region was number one within two years.

Meanwhile, I spread my wings, stepped on toes, and made enemies faster than I made friends. I loved every minute of it. The only real problem was that I lived in Memphis and didn't have a Texas license plate on my car. In 1985, Steve offered me a shot at the national sales manager's job. The home office was in Rochester, New York. I hadn't lost anything up there so I declined. That was the beginning of the end of my eighteen year run. I retired from Fisons Limited at the age of fifty-seven.

I needed a few more years to qualify for social security and teacher retirement, so I spent four years as the chief operations and disciplinarian officer of a central Texas elementary school. At no time did I expect to stay more than another year but the weekly commute lasted four long years. The only people in the school that I really liked were the kids, and the only kids I dealt with were the hostiles.

In June of 1996, fate set me free after forty years of working for others. I retired for good. I was born for it. Sixteen years, four books, and the busiest and best time in my life followed.

Earl Stubbs—2012

Earl Stubbs

Part IV

BITS AND PIECES OF A LIFE

23

If we cannot secure all our rights, let us secure what we can—Thomas Jefferson

THE ORIGIN OF TEARS
1936

Do I actually recall any of these episodes or do they evolve from lore relayed to me over the decades from a variety of sources?

I suspect that the latter prevails. It is not likely that I remember too much, since I was twenty-three months old at the time. However, patches of light, transient images, the pungent smell of sachet and urine, and the sounds of strident voices dominate my recollections.

The event was the funeral of Willie Gertrude Hampton Stubbs. She passed at the age of thirty-one leaving a young husband and three children of which I was the youngest. Joining me on this day of dispersal were my two sisters. Dorothy Jean was six, and Marvalynn eleven.

Compelling Journey

In those days, family members involved themselves in the affairs of other members, especially, during times of severe illness. When the local physician hospitalized our mother in Texarkana, her sister Opal, reluctantly, assumed my care. I say this because of a postcard from Aunt Opal to another family member that survived. In the letter, she stated that caring for me was an imposition. However, she was kind enough to bring me to the funeral.

It was as if the death of a good woman was a minor scene in the play. The major players in this drama were James Madison Stubbs, age seventy-seven, his daughter, Ella Clyde Stubbs Price, age fifty-three, and Marvin Lester Stubbs, age thirty-six, his son and our father.

Grandpa played the puppet master. Marvin, known within the family as Poor Marvin, had a walk-on role. Ella Clyde co-starred as a female Machiavelli. My sisters and I played supporting cast members with non-speaking roles.

James Madison Stubbs had a number of names, including Pa, Uncle Jim, Grandpa, and Mr. Jim. He was a whisky drinking, fist-fighting, patriarch, who ruled with an iron hand. Grandpa had a still that produced white lightening. His reputation implied that he would cut you.

Ella Clyde was a chipess off the old block. She could talk the horns off a billy goat and was as mean as a snake. Only Grandpa had any influence on Eller, as family members called her.

Earl Stubbs

Poor Marvin gained his family name because of his brushes with death and his current predicament. He was the baby of the family, had survived the 1918 flu, had survived a burst appendix, and had lost his beloved wife. He was not a major player in this drama. Grandpa and Eller had already written the scenario and left him out.

A logical, albeit selfish goal motivated Grandpa. He was 77 years old and his best days long gone. As was the culture of the day, he cared for his son, Corbon Edgar, a severe epileptic and demented soul. After the death of our Grandmother Lucy, Grandpa married a neighboring widow, Olie Knight, and added to his land pool. She did not live long.

He needed Marvin to do the heavy lifting, lead the singing on Sunday, feed the mules, farm the forty acres, feed the stock, and serve as a hunting and fishing buddy. Grandpa would make the biscuits, the white lightening, and call the shots. It was a hell of a deal for everyone except Marvin's three children.

Eller's incentive was primitive. She had lost an infant son when she was young. She had one troubled daughter, Ella Mae Price Barker, but that was not nearly enough for the family gatherings. She needed a son, and providence placed one within her grasp. It was only a matter of being forceful and clever. She was both.

Marvin was in the process of burying his decision maker and needed someone to manage his affairs. He had a sharecrop to harvest, no money, hospital bills, and

Compelling Journey

no backbone. If he could get someone to raise his children, without it costing him anything, he was way ahead of the game. I never said he was dumb.

Marvin enjoyed the farm life. He preferred working hard to make and bring in a crop, leading the singing at the church on Sunday, playing a little baseball, and then chilling-out for the rest of the year.

After the burial, Eller casually slid over to Aunt Opal and offered to hold me for a minute. Once that simple act occurred, she never gave me back. Lives changed forever. Eller proclaimed that she would look after my sisters and me for a while. There were no dissenters or counter offers. We piled in Ella Mae's husband, John L. Barker's Plymouth, and drove from the Flat Creek Cemetery in Cass County to a white house by the railroad tracks in Mt. Pleasant, Texas.

Here is how matters played out. Eller, who became Mama to me for the remainder of her life, rid herself of my sisters after about six months. I spent my formative years with the Price family, and then went off to college. My foster-sister/cousin, Ella Mae, furnished the money at great sacrifice to herself.

Various family members and would-be foster parents separated the girls, passed them around for a year or more, but then they ended up with a childless couple who had an enormous interest in school teaching and the hereafter. Unfortunately, this was after damage to their psyche was done. They lived less than ten miles

Earl Stubbs

from me in Naples, but I can count on one hand the number of times my sisters and I visited as we grew up.

Grandpa brought in another wife. Her name was Miss Anne Richerson, but she didn't last long either. Uncle Edgar, the epileptic, passed soon after her. Grandpa passed soon after that. Marvin hurt his back on the farm or so the story goes. Mama drove down and brought him home with her. I clearly recall the reunion with my long-lost father. He spoke oddly and smelled to high heaven.

Marvin worked in a small grocery store for a few months, and then he got a job at Red River Arsenal in Texarkana. After the war, he launched a career selling Raleigh Products door to door ... mostly to poor black families. He moved out as soon as possible, remarried later, and spent the rest of his life in the area.

When he lost his health and income, his second wife of twenty years, Bonnie Rui Mckinny Stubbs, lost her empathy and asked my sisters to come get Marvin. They shared the role of caretakers for about a year. One kept him for a few weeks and then the other. Finally, for reasons best explained by them, they asked me to alleviate the problem. I placed Marvin in the Rosebud Nursing Home in Naples. He couldn't understand why we wouldn't care for him in our homes. He didn't like it at Rosebud.

Compelling Journey

24

If a house be divided against itself, that house cannot stand.--The Gospel of Mark

THE HOUSE BY THE TRACKS
1936

Age three

Everyone must have a starting place for a conscious life and Mt. Pleasant, Texas, was mine. A busy rail center in the late thirties, local steam engines switched freight, coal, and tank cars into units for diversion to their destinations. They emitted short, strident blasts on their steam whistles, while the long haulers gave off extended, lonesome sounds at all hours of the day or night. Being accustomed to the environment, the noise became less disruptive to our everyday lives. On occasion, when the house shook, and it seemed that the engineer would never turn loose of the horn cord, one stopped what he or she was doing and waited for the racket to abate.

The white house sat on an area level with the tracks; then the lot dropped off about ten feet on the north and east sides of the property forming something of a moat. A large tree sat near the drop-off and was ideal for my old tire swing that took me out over the precipice.

One of the main streets from downtown Mt. Pleasant bordered the south side of our rented land. The tracks sat on the west boundary and separated our house from the main business district of Mt. Pleasant.

The location of our house was of major importance. We ran a rooming house for railway personnel, while they awaited their next trip. While I am certain that my mind plays tricks, I remember the tracks to be no more than twenty yards from the side of our house. When railroads dominated transportation, the giant, steam-driven locomotives rolled past with regularity. They exuded authority and noise. The freight trains appeared of interminable length as they swayed past. The long line of colorful boxcars with a variety of identifications ended

Compelling Journey

with the ubiquitous red caboose. The entire rail industry was one of power and romance.

I recall two neighbors. One was a person of German origin named Hines. He had a colorful peacock in his yard and brewed wine. We purchased small bottles of home-brewed wine from him on rare occasions, so he produced the first alcoholic beverage to pass my lips. I call to mind the sharp taste. Mr. Hines' place in the neighborhood evolved to infamy as the thirties played out and, according to local gossip, he became a Nazi spy.

A bevy of beautiful Latino women lived across the street to the south. Our frequent visitor was Juanita. We visited back and forth and kept up with family gossip. They treated us to the best tamales known to man on the occasions that we requested them.

Except for the rare visit from family friends who had small children, I had only two playmates during the four years I lived in the house by the tracks. One came over with his mother on a couple of occasions. We returned the visit. His house had a goldfish pond in the front yard. I liked playing with the boy and many years later, we attended college together.

One of the reasons we lived in this house was because it had a storm cellar. The cool, dark cavern offered a great place for imaginary games and for luring a visiting little girl of my age down there for our first game of playing doctor. Unfortunately, we were unable to conclude our examinations, before her mother interrupted us and suggested that we put on our clothes.

There was a front porch on the north side with a swing. With an inspired imagination, I could turn the north/south swing into an east/west locomotive complete with the proper sound effects. When the little girl came back to visit, we transferred our medical practice to the swing with the same result. Really! How much damage can a curious five-year-old do?

A lack of basic equipment forced me toward creativity in the area of personal entertainment. In addition to the tire swing, the exterior of the house provided other important areas that contributed to my amusement. Having several tiny cars from Christmases past, I prepared a series of roads in a sandy area behind the back porch that provided countless hours of play. The most important part of the exterior of the house was the chimney, my most dependable playmate.

I could not have been much more than four when I first tried to play catch with myself. Ella Mae's husband, John L., had a brother, who had played professional baseball, and he had one of his brother's cast-off fielder's glove. In addition, I had an old tennis ball and a vivid imagination. I placed the glove on one of my tiny hands, and took the ball in the other. In the beginning, it didn't matter which hand held the ball, nor did it matter that I could put my entire hand in any of the fingers of the

Compelling Journey

glove. I needed to figure out whether I was right-handed or left-handed through trial and error.

I learned to throw and catch. At some point, I discovered that the glove didn't help. After eliminating my left arm as a contender, throwing with my right arm came quickly. Catching the ball did not, but over the months, I was able to seize just about every ball I threw against the chimney. I can't recall anything in my young life that provided more good times than throwing that old, dead tennis ball against the chimney and then catching it. It was during those formative times that I developed my love for physical games.

A lowlight during our stay in the house by the tracks was a trip to the barbershop. I was four years old. Not only did I hate being still for so long, but on that day, one could literally fry an egg on the street. After the haircut, Mama and I started back to our home no more than a hundred yards to the East. I was barefoot and decided about halfway across a series of burning railroad tracks that I could not put my feet on the pavement. Standing in place, I lifted one foot then the other and vociferously alerted the world that I was unhappy with this environmental imperfection. To add to the quandary, a train approached. Mama had already traversed the street, and she loitered on the other side encouraging me. She didn't help me, but she encouraged me. Finally, as the freight train's whistle blared, I chose life over death, hopped across the tracks, and endured Mama's diatribe until we got home. Don't ask me why that predicament became my fault, because I can't answer your question.

25

A person is never happy except at the price of some ignorance—Anatole France

FIRST CHRISTMAS 1938

On the first Christmas that I recall, I received a red electric train complete with track, passenger cars, and a caboose. It ran around a small oval, until it built up speed, and then it jumped the track, but I didn't care. I would put it back and begin the process once more.

My second most important gift that year was a small, chocolate brown doll. Don't ask me why a five-year-old boy with no discernable feminine tendencies, would receive a doll for Christmas, but many things that I couldn't explain occurred during those times. Though I never played with the doll, except to check out her anatomy, we kept Molly around for many years. In fact, she made her way to the storage trunk, which only held important items, such as crochet dollies grayed with age that would never see the light of day.

Earl Stubbs

In addition to the big-ticket items, I received small cars and trucks that I enjoyed for a long time. Building roads for my little cars provided many hours of contentment. I received the ubiquitous oranges, apples, and various unshelled nuts. Unfortunately, the shelling proved more troublesome than the enjoyment of the end product. One nut was usually enough. Stockings and their contents had to be a carryover from the middle ages.

The key to the 1938 Christmas was that it was the first one that I can really remember. I was eager, my foster-family was excited, and the quality of the gifts was super. During the next seventy-seven years, the joy of Christmas never came close.

Due to the needs of World War II, metal was unavailable for toys, so the guns I needed for play during those years were often made of sawdust. Every year, I would get up on Christmas morning and expect to repeat the thrill of 1938, but it has never happened.

Compelling Journey

26

**The mob has many heads but no brains.--
Thomas Fuller**

STATIC
1939

One cannot live by imagination alone. There are times when one requires association with other humans, no matter how cantankerous or mean-spirited they are. Before World War II, the one thing that drew families together was the radio, and I was no different. The radio provided entertainment. I needed it then, and I need it now.

During 1938, the news turned dark, and I began listening to the big folks discuss world events. While no one in our immediate family expected to go across the ocean, aunts and uncles had several male members available for the draft. Tensions ran high. My Aunt Valary could wax philosophically for long periods on Old Jaypan, Old Hitler, and Old Mussolini. She had two sons, Royce and Ben, who were prime candidates to defend our country.

Earl Stubbs

Ben joined the Works Progress Administration, a stimulus work program designed to break the depression. Being immature, he got homesick and came home. Eventually, the county board drafted him into the infantry. As it turned out, he served under General Patton with bravery and distinction all the way from Utah Beach in Normandy to Germany's surrender.

Royce was a musician and wrote poetry. The army examination discovered a perforated eardrum and declared him 4F. There were scores of perforated eardrums in those days.

*****

The first radio broadcast was in 1906, and the technonogy became important in World War I. The military used radios in air and naval operations. Detroit broadcast the first radio news program on August 31, 1920. KDKA in Pittsburgh was the first commercial radio station. President Wilson used radio during the last part of his presidency. By 1922, a million sets were in use.

Early radio shows included adventure, comedy, drama, horror, mystery, musical variety, romance, news, quiz shows, talent shows, and weather predictions. Orchestras played in the 30s and 40s. Arturo Toscanini directed the NBC Symphony Orchestra. George Gershwin was a frequent guest and had his own program in 1934. Country music found a place with the National

Compelling Journey

Barn Dance (Chicago) in 1924. It took on the name of the Grand Ol Opry in 1927.

Many of the stars of vaudeville comedy pioneered radio. Bob Hope, Milton Berle, Jack Benny, Red Skelton, and George Burns & Gracie Allen made the transition from vaudeville to radio to television. Most women had their favorite soap operas. They were not a guy thing. Mama and Ellie controlled the radio dial at our house during the daytime. We listened to Young Widow Brown, Lorenzo Jones, Stella Dallas, Ma Perkins, and Our Gal Sunday. Our Miss Brooks was a nighttime favorite. Rinso, Oxydol, Dreft, Ivory Soap, and Palmolive sponsored these classic representations of life during the Great Depression.

Two powerful stations in Dallas, KRLD and WFAA, sent out their signals to East Texas. On some days, static was so bad, we could hardly follow the vital conversations in progress. The stations cut back on power at night, so the background noise increased. Weather was an important factor as well.

I cannot recall the story lines from any of the programs, but I do recollect that the women in the title roles always spoke with kindness and reason, while their adversaries sounded strident and backbiting. The organ music in the background added greatly to the entertainment value.

Family members established ownership of the shows and each referred to them as my programs. Both Mama and Ellie spent considerable time analyzing each episode, as to what they would have done had they been involved. Stating the obvious was the norm of the day. Referring to the bad women as old heifers occurred with regularity.

Two radio events made an indelible impression on me during those years in Mt. Pleasant. The first was the heavyweight championship fight between the current champion, Joe Louis from the USA, and the former champion, Max Schmeling from Germany.

Numerous factors endorsed the fight. Going back to WWI, Germany was the Western world's archenemy. Promoters billed the fight as a battle between good and evil, a struggle between the USA and Germany, and black versus white. To compound matters, the two fighters had met in 1936 in New York. Before that fight, Schmeling confessed to having found a weakness in Louis' style. It seemed that Louis dropped his guard after throwing a punch. He capitalized on the theory and knocked Louis down early in the fight. He went on to knock Louis out in the twelfth round. Winning back the belt was not enough, America wanted revenge against the German.

I recall that the call of the fight came and went. Static overpowered the speakers for a bit, and then the voices came back. My attention span being short at the age of four, it is fortunate that the fight was a short one. I do recall that Joe Louis knocked out Schmeling in the first round. I guess he didn't drop his guard that time.

Compelling Journey

After WWII, Schmeling obtained the Coca Cola franchise in Germany and became a rich man. He and Louis met in person twelve times during later years. He spent considerable money on Louis during his destitute days and served as a pallbearer at his funeral. Schmeling lived to be ninety-nine and was a good friend of Lawrence McNamee, the legendary German professor at ET.

The next radio show that got the attention of not only me, but the country as a whole, occurred in 1938 as well. It was a clear night in October. Ellie's husband, John L., took a night off from the honky tonk circuit and listened to the Mercury Theatre. The show started as usual, and then suddenly, an officious sounding voice came on saying that the network was interrupting regular programming for breaking news. Major cities came under attack from unidentified beings in strange airships. The radio reporters soon learned that Martians were the attackers and the damage was spreading.

The family abandoned the radio and went outside to see if we could see any Martian spaceships. The warm, calm evening produced no marauding invaders. Other people in the neighborhood were outside as well.

John L., who remained glued to the radio, came out of the house and declared that the program was over. It was a hoax. Mama wrapped up the incident by saying, "You can't believe anything you hear on that old radio. They didn't fool me for a minute."

Earl Stubbs

Compelling Journey

27

If our house be on fire, without enquiring whether it was fired from within or without, we must try to extinguish it.--Thomas Jefferson

OLD UNION
1940

I worshiped the memory of my sisters. My most prized possession was a snapshot of them I kept hidden in a cigar box. I was not aware of their whereabouts after they left Mama's house, but I had only to get out the photograph to refresh my memory of their existence.

Relatives and acquaintances of the family separated the girls and passed my younger sister, Dorothy, around from house to house for about a year. Then she landed in the bottom of the pit when her benefactors relocated her to Grandpa Jim's house along with Marvin, demented Edward, and a host of chinch bugs.

Marvalynn, the eldest, stayed for a time with a judge and his wife. They wanted to adopt her, but she would have none of it. Finally, Old Jim made his final contribution to their lives. He arranged for both Dorothy and Marvalynn to live with a couple of good Christian schoolteachers who lived a few miles away in Marietta. The lives of my sisters improved immeasurably from that point.

*****

Mama's neuralgia took on life-threatening proportions after John L. left, and she grew weary of Ella Mae rehashing the conditions of the breakup. It became time to move. She chose a small house behind the Old Union Baptist Church a few miles east of Mt. Pleasant.

Again, there were virtually no neighbors, so my entertainment was my own. That consisted of playing with my little dog Penny and my goat Billy. Penny got on Mama's nerves, so she found her another home. I played with Billy one day and fell. Mama thought he was attacking me, so she came to the rescue. Billy hooked her thumb with his sharp horns and cut a blood vessel. He was history in a matter of hours.

My primary source of amusement was a BB gun. I shot everything that moved and hit nothing, but the possibility was always there.

Soon, I was six, and it was time to take a major step toward my future. I was not delighted at the prospect of going to school that first day. The most troublesome aspect being that I had a name problem. Mama called me Bud. Ellie, called me Buddy. Uncle Dud was Mama's

Compelling Journey

husband. He provided the money for the car and the vagabond lifestyle preferred by Mama. When he was home for the occasional weekend, he referred to me as Buck. With all of that, Mama had informed me that when the teacher asked my name, I was to say Earl. Only my sisters called me that ... actually, they called me Earl Wayne on the rare occasions when I saw them.

On the other hand, I anticipated one major reward for going to school. I would learn to read. I would no longer have to beg and plead to family members to read me the funnies. It never ceased to amaze me how busy everyone became on Sunday morning when the paper arrived. Having no pride where Mandrake the Magician was concerned, I would trudge from person to person, beseeching, imploring, and stooping to any degradation to get someone to read me the funnies. I could get the main story line from the pictures, but I just had to know what Mandrake was saying to Lothar. In most instances, I never found out. I practiced Mandrake's hand action for hours, but I could never get anything to disappear no matter how hard I tried.

*****

I could smell the newness of my unwashed overalls that bright September morning in 1940. They were striped blue and white with a loop for a hammer on the right leg. Mama held tightly to my hand, guiding me around the puddles left from last night's rain.

"Now Bud, pay attention to me. You look both ways before you cross that highway. If there ain't no cars coming, you run for dear life. You're too little to go to school anyway. Pay attention to me Bud?"

I nodded while gazing ahead at the white frame building with the Bell tower in front. The school sat only about two hundred yards down the sandy road from our house. The only obstacles between the two were the Old Union Baptist Church and US highway 67, which curved in front of the Old Union community school. This less than thriving community sat a few miles east of Mt. Pleasant in northeast Texas. The speed limit on the highway was thirty-five mph in 1940 and traffic was light. The possibility of danger was mostly a product of Mama's hyperactive nervous system.

Mama chattered nonstop since we had left home for school. When we reached the highway, there was not a car in sight. "Look both ways," Mama shouted, dashing for the other side of the highway and dragging me along. By this time, my apprehension had grown somewhat. The students that I could see on the school yard appeared to be much bigger than me and a surly lot as well. Unmoved, Mama went charging up the front stairs with me in tow and barreled down the hall to one of the rooms at the back of the four-room building.

Compelling Journey

She went straight up to a woman who appeared to be an authority figure. We learned that my teacher was Mrs. Toliver, and she was in the process of comforting another first day scholar. The student was teary-eyed and twice a big as me. He refused to turn loose of his mother's hand. Mama, not one to stand on formality, moved between the teacher and the problem child and stated with some firmness, "This is Earl Stubbs. He is going to be in the primer. He is little and sickly. Don't let him sit in the wind. When school is out, take him across the highway." Then she turned to me, "Now Bud, you behave yourself."

Mrs. Toliver almost but not quite managed to keep her mouth closed as she stared at Mama's departing figure. However, she quickly regained her composure and directed me to a seat on the front row. For me, formal education began.

Fortunately, the system in place only lost the first half of the school day. After our teacher established logistics, she gave instructions for study. Most students knew what to do. They whipped out books and writing instruments and applied them to the task at hand. I could find nothing that faintly resembled the supplies of my neighbors. By noon, I discovered that the room held not one but three grades.

After a lunch made memorable by a scarlet mush of tomatoes and grits, and because of my inability to eat even one bite, Mrs. Rice summoned me. She inquired as to whether or not I knew the alphabet. I proudly responded in the affirmative. Surprisingly, she picked me up and placed me on her lap. Then she chose a small thin book and opened it. The title was **Spot and Jane**. She pointed to a word, spelled it, and then pronounced it. After repeating the process with all the words in the first line, she asked me to try. I did so, and she appeared pleased with my results. After a few pages, she requested that I try to progress on my own. Without realizing it, I achieved the first step toward solving the mystery of reading the Sunday funnies.

Later in the day, an event brought me to the attention of the rest of the student body. It concerned the large iron school Bell that hung in front of the building. Acutely aware of the activities of other students, I noticed that after the Bell sounded signaling the end of morning recess, everyone made a mad dash to line up in front of the steps. After observing the same phenomenon again at lunch, I concluded that both the bell ringer and the first in line acquired status among the students. By the time the afternoon recess was just about half over, I formulated a plan by which I could ring the bell and also be first in line. I sidled up to the tower, grasp the rope, and tugged with all my limited might. The bell started to ring. I quickly abandoned the rope and lined up in front of the steps. The other students lined behind me without question. About the time everyone was ready to march into the school, out walked a tall, spare man with a stern

Compelling Journey

countenance. He intently peered at a old pocket watch. He approached the group and made inquiries.

Soon, fingers pointed in my direction, and the tall man extended his hand to me. I took it, and he led me aside. We proceeded to have a one-sided conversation regarding the ringing of the school bell. I felt cooperative at the time, so I promised not to repeat my error in judgment. Relieved that my first day at school was a learning experience, he smiled as he walked away.

Later in the afternoon that cursed bell rang out signaling the end of the school day. Mrs. Toliver took me by the hand and marched me to the edge of the highway. Mama was perched on the other side looking frantic. Along came a dilapidated model A Ford, gasping for every chug. We watched it pass. Then the three of us went through the exaggerated ritual of looking first one way, then the other. As the roadway was obviously clear, Mrs. Toliver turned loose my hand, and I sprinted across the asphalt strip. Without acknowledging my teacher, Mama grasp my hand and charged away filling the warm afternoon with invective.

*****

Soon, we reached the white frame house that was our current home. Mama had a way of justifying the moves. Usually, we would stay in a new situation only long enough for her to become bored with the neighbors at which time her vitality faltered and a move for the sake of her health resulted.

On this day, however, Mama and I entered the house by the kitchen door and found Ellie seated at the table nursing the ever present cup of coffee. She wore, as was her pattern, a faded print dress that was in shreds. It was not that she didn't own better clothing. Her mode of dress was one of her many ploys intended to extract sympathy. The fact that her repugnant appearance just might earn disgust rather than pity never occurred to Ellie. She had only just uttered her favorite dictum which was, "I'll stomp more hell out of her in a minute than she can gather up in a week. Buddy, how did you like school? Mama, I'm going to town to find that bitch."

I mumbled an answer, laid down my books, and went looking for my untrustworthy air rifle. Not to be denied, Ellie shouted from the kitchen, "Buddy, I'm all tore up. Come and read these coffee grounds. I saw a bird at the winder awhile ago, and I'm scared something bad is going to happen." There was no escape, so I parked my gun and slouched back into the kitchen. I intended to make this fast and brutal.

Ellie's mode of existence consisted of preparing, drinking, or staring at black coffee of the vilest sort. In addition, she kept up a constant dialogue with Mama concerning the status of her marriage to her, here today gone tomorrow, husband, John L. It made for lively albeit redundant conversation.

Compelling Journey

Johnny was no real problem for me, except that he was just another family member who would not read me the Sunday funnies. I always knew where I stood with him. I did not exist. Actually, I preferred him to worrisome Ellie who would whine to any warm body within earshot, age not withstanding. After thirteen years of a marital joke, Johnny discovered honky tonks, spirits, and hussies in that order, and he was making up for lost time.

A few months earlier, when we lived in town and Johnny could find a bar with little effort, the home situation became untenable. One day after Ellie tore off her dress, because Johnny wanted her to buy a new one, he informed the ladies that he would find other lodging. For the first few days, the only course of action was raging overt indignation and threats from Ellie and Mama. Finally, they both realized that Johnny was not there to hear them, and we had heard it all before. So, they chose a more compromising approach resulting in simpering servility. Forays into town became the order of the day seeking John L.'s elusive car. About a week later, much to my surprise, Johnny returned. Unfortunately, I made the egregious error of mentioning that I had sought and probably received divine assistance in securing his return. After that, I became the resident ear of God and chief coffee ground reader. My services in both areas were to be frequently requested, because this was not to be Johnny's last venture outside the bosom of his family.

Ellie drained the cup and flipped it over. She turned it three times in the gritty saucer making the most frightful noise. After she stopped, it was necessary to wait three silent minutes for the spirits to do their work. While waiting, I practiced sighting my rifle. Lord only knows, I needed the practice. Finally, she turned the cup over and slid it across the table to me.

To be honest, I never had the faintest notion about what I was supposed to see in the coffee grounds. Usually, I came up with something inoffensive such as travel or money. This time, since I was a bit miffed, I chose to be more creative. I gazed into the cup for a long moment. Ellie, unable to control her curiosity, ask, "What do you see, Buddy?"

I looked up gravely from the cup squeezing a solitary tear from the corner of my eye. "Somebody is going to be sick," I proclaimed. Mama looked profound and uttered somberly, "Bud knows stuff." I could immediately sense that Mama was not altogether displeased. Illness was the major topic of conversation at the family gatherings, and Mama had been disgustingly healthy for years. Although she had tried to die since the age of thirty from various aches and pains, she gradually lost status at the

Compelling Journey

family gatherings. She had commanded no real respect since her hysterectomy of some fifteen years previously.

Ellie was not so easily mollified. She was interested in information regarding the sluts and whores that constantly tempted John L. away from his happy home. When she began to grumble, I gazed at the coffee grounds and threw her a bone.

"Somebody is going to move far away." I figured it was going to be us since we had been at the same place for over six months. Ellie interpreted this revelation to mean that either John L. was going to depart permanently or that she and Johnny were going to go it "on our own." We all knew that Mama would never allow the latter to happen. Neither Ellie nor Mama was suited for life without the other.

After lengthy interpretation of the reading, I was dismissed. As I left, I could hear the spirited dialogue. It consisted of Ellie using Mama as a non-responding sounding board regarding Ellie's problems and solutions to those problems. At the same time, Mama bounced sage wisdom off Ellie who never heard a word she said.

I trudged out into the late afternoon sunlight and headed for the sandy road. Fortunately, those who had cleared the land that bordered the road left tall native elm trees along the right-of-way. Ancient sentinels, they provided home and shelter for a variety of winged creatures and squirrels. The foliage was so thick that branches from trees on the west side grew to intermingle with branches on the east side forming a barrier to the sun. Even on the brightest day, the lane was dark and gloomy due to the tunnel of elms. Farther to the north the ruts disappeared over a rise. My vivid imagination invented a variety of dire circumstances must lurk past the dark road, so I was never brave enough to really take a look.

Certain that the animals accepted the fact that I was completely harmless, I still faithfully launched missile after missile toward those feathered brutes while enduring their chirping scorn.

Compelling Journey

After a time highlighted by my lack of success, Mama began to call. The birds ceased chirping in fear. I started my saunter back toward the house, hurling insults at my adversaries.

When I reached the house and entered the back door, Mama set me to work on my numbers. I was up to eight when she announced supper. A glance at the table confirmed my suspicions that there was absolutely nothing there that I could abide. Nevertheless, we began.

Mama and Ellie could have conversations that lasted for days with one discussing one subject and the other embroiled in something else entirely. On this occasion Ellie entertained with alternate crying jags and cursing fits. Mama, never one to let a full mouth stand in the way of oratory, offered advice as to what she would do if she were in Ellie's place. Poor Ellie had no doubt as to what Mama would do. Mama had been doing it to Uncle Dud for 35 years. What Ellie did not know was what she was going to do. As for myself, no one appeared to care that boiled turnips would not go down my throat.

28

**Anger is a signal and one worth listening to—
Harriet Lerner**

THE SHOOTING
1940

Nothing much changed for the next few months. Johnny came around and stayed for a few days, until the two women abandoned the olive branch and launched a counteroffensive, then he disappeared again. I tried the divine assistance game a few more times, but there was so much coming and going, that I really couldn't tell if it was working or not. I figured that even if it was, I couldn't expect to keep getting all of that spiritual personal attention forever. It was difficult to determine whether Ellie carried on more when Johnny was gone or when he was home. I really didn't care much anymore. By this time, with the exception of the occasional word, I could read the funnies to myself.

* * * * *

Compelling Journey

The bitter north wind was heavy with moisture that sullen afternoon in December. I no longer required assistance in crossing highway 67, and Mama had long since ceased coming to meet me. It interfered with one of her naps. I hurried down the road as the wind bit through my thin trousers. Nearing the house, I noticed a strange car in the drive. John L. was laughing and talking to some people through the window of the car. I stopped when I saw Ellie come out of the house waving John L.'s old .38 pistol and cursing a blue streak. She pointed the gun toward the car and pulled the trigger repeatedly. The shots made dull thumping sounds.

The driver of the car hurriedly backed out of the drive and headed my way. I moved off the road, as the vehicle roared past. I heard people yelling inside the car.

Ellie dropped the gun, fell to the ground, and began sobbing. John L. picked up the gun and stared at it. Then, he tossed it back on the ground, got in his car, and charged off leaving a trail of exhaust. Ellie struggled to her feet and called for mama.

I found myself in a quandary. I couldn't face going home and dealing with the scene there. I couldn't return to school. I needed time to process this new situation. Shooting was different, and it frightened me. After all, I had seen what Tom Mix could do with a gun.

Earl Stubbs

I needed to make a decision. I could go in the house and deal with the insanity there, or I could find out what was over the darkened road to the north. Due to the thick clouds and gloom, the country path through the tunnel of elms appeared exceptionally dark that day, but for some reason, it didn't look so bad. I made my choice, fastened my aviator cap under my chin, and dropped the glasses over my eyes. I walked past the house and tossed my book satchel into the yard. Then, I began walking into the frigid and quickening breath of the north wind.

I walked for what seemed a long time. Much to my surprise, the road past the rise was pretty much the same as on this side. I felt no yearning to return home, so I kept walking. As dusk approached, the dimness increased along with the cold. My light coat was not getting it done, so when I came upon a small creek with a culvert, I decided to get out of the wind. There was plenty of room under the road for me to rest for a while. I sat down and bundled up to ward off the freezing air. I began getting drowsy and soon slipped off to sleep.

The baying of hounds was the first thing that woke me. My teeth chattering, I soon discovered that I was freezing cold. Soon, something wet touched my face in the form of the long tongue of a hound dog. Within a minute, strong hands lifted me from the culvert and wrapped me in blankets. I don't recall much about the trip back home, but I do remember feeling the warmth of the feather bed overcome the discomfort of the cold as I drifted away.

Weapon used in the shooting.

* * * * *

School became a matter of routine. I completed a few arithmetic assignments during the morning or listened to the older kids recite. Usually, when everyone else was busy, Mrs. Rice sat me on her lap, and I would read in one of those little books. Eventually, she informed me that I would move up a grade after Christmas. I was learning to appreciate my time at school, not so much for what I did there, but due to the fact that it was time away from the emotional roller coaster of home.

The absence of John L. and Mama's declining health forced us to move away from the Old Union community just before Christmas. My school experiences in 1940 ceased when we moved back to Mt. Pleasant. Mama didn't like to be alone with Ellie all of the time, besides, according to Mama, the students at the elementary school two blocks away from our house were mean. I started over again in Naples the following school year after another move for reasons of health. Except for the absence of John L., our household changed little until I left for college twelve years later. Ella Mae worked hard as a waitress and nurse. Mama continued as Mama. Uncle Dud spent more time at home due to the short distance, and he eventually retired to his cigarettes and emphasyma. He made one final contribution to my life. I joined the army, but he begged me not go go. I didn't and it altered my life in a major way—for the better I believe.

Compelling Journey

29

Mere precedent is a dangerous source of authority--Andrew Jackson

SPANKY
1941

It was December of 1940. John L. had joyfully departed for California. Ellie was inconsolable, and Mama's health required a modification in her surroundings, so she pulled me out of school, and we moved back to Mt. Pleasant. I lost the school year, the promotion at midterm, and the state advancement of one grade for everyone. Not putting me back in school in 1940 did not lose me one school year. It lost me three. As it turned out, that was a good thing. I was still small and immature when I started over in 1941.

The Weems family owned an icehouse in Mt. Pleasant, located across the street from our new rent house. Big Buck Weems operated the business. Though this information is purely speculation, the family must have nicknamed the youngest sibling after the roly-poly member of the movie shorts, *Our Gang*. Demonstrating many of the same physical traits as the movie version, Spanky Weems was heavy and had a round freckled face. He was loud and aggressive as well.

Spanky discovered me the first weekend, after we abandoned the Old Union Community and settled into our new retreat. I was six, and he must have been nine or ten. He decided that I would do for occasional recreation even though I was younger and quite small. Quickly taking advantage of the opportunities provided by the icehouse, we stood around and watched as Buck and his hired hand dispensed blocks of ice to waiting customers. We also retrieved the dropped slivers of ice and crunched our fill, which didn't take long at that time of the year. When someone opened the door to the dark interior of the ice storage area, glacial fog drifted out. Spanky took me inside, and we experienced the savage cold for a short time. It was always a relief to me when we regained the safety and comfort of the outside.

Spanky and I found other ways to amuse ourselves after school and on the weekends. While he was boisterous, he was not cruel. He introduced me to kite building. We made them from sticks tied together with twine, old newspapers, and glue made from flour and water. The weight of the kite, after the glue dried enough to keep the kite together, must have approached that of

Compelling Journey

lead. Consequently, we had much fun building kites but little success flying them.

The rubber band gun provided a homemade toy that was more useful. It required a piece of wood, shaped like a long pistol, to which we attached a clothespin to the grip. Held securely by the clothespin, we stretched a thin strip of automobile or bicycle tube around the other end. When we pressed the clothespin, the rubber missile would fly a short distance with some velocity.

A more dangerous weapon was the rock shooter made from a Y-shaped stock. We attached two thin strips of rubber to the fork, and then we connected the two strips with a piece of leather. The latter was usually the tongue from a discarded shoe. Next, we placed a rock in the leather pouch, pulled the rock back as far as possible, and let it fly. These devices could launch rocks a considerable distance. It is interesting to note that we instinctively knew not to shoot at one another with these weapons.

We had a grand old time when Spanky was around. However, being a naive soul, I thought that the icehouse was available to me when he wasn't, so I began hanging out with Buck and the boys while Spanky was at school. I did not take the hint when Buck barked at me to get out of the way.

Earl Stubbs

Being my obstructive self one day, Buck casually invited me into the ice storage room. It occurred to me he was a true friend. I went right in and began seeking a prized sliver of ice. Then, to my complete shock, the door slammed shut. Adjusting to the absolute absence of light, I just stood there. Then, the cold commenced permeating my clothes and I panicked. At first, I nicely requested that Buck open the door, but that method rapidly evolved into me screaming bloody murder.

After what seemed time without end, the door opened. I fled the dark interior and rushed into the sunlight. Buck invited me to get on my side of the street and stay there. He wasted his breath. A team of elephants could not have dragged me back to that icehouse, with or without Spanky. I, seamlessly, transferred my attention back to my imaginary friends and played alone.

*****

While we lived in Old Union, Mama's husband, Uncle Dud Price, gave me a single-shot BB gun. There were many opportunities to shoot the gun out in the country, but when we moved back to Mt. Pleasant, there were few. Of course, I fired it indoors on occasion, but the family did not encourage that. Always on the lookout for a creative means to spice up my dreary life, I noticed a

Compelling Journey

case of empty Coke bottles in the neighbor's back yard. It occurred to me that one could break a glass vessel only once, but if several were available, I could extend the fun.

After convincing myself that no one was looking, I set up a shooting range. At the short distance involved, I broke bottle after bottle marveling at my marksmanship. I enjoyed myself immensely, until I looked up into the eyes of the woman who lived in the house next door. She was not pleased with my sporting activity. Having no moral leg to stand on, I swiftly retreated indoors.

Regardless, the woman next door and Mama had a conference. The foundation of the treaty arranged between the two was that I would pay for the broken bottles and apologize. For some reason, the thought of acting contrite was more than I could bear. Regret was not a part of my young psychological makeup. I pleaded, begged, implored, and outright refused to carry out my part of the bargain, but to no avail. In those days, Mama was still in charge, so I skulked next door and completed my punishment. It was a learning experience.

Though I did not realize it at the time, the story remained incomplete for an additional sixty-seven years. During a conversation with a nice man named Ed from Lindale, Texas, I learned that we knew people in common. For some reason, we stumbled onto the knowledge that when we lived across from the icehouse

Earl Stubbs

in Mt. Pleasant, the woman next door was his aunt. Ed shared with me that her husband was one of the local bootleggers. The empty Coke bottles were containers for selling Sugar Hill White Lightening. Little did I know that even at that young age, I was fighting crime for life, liberty, and the pursuit of justice.

1923 Dec. 25 | 1937 Aug. 3 (D-105529) | 1957 Applied Color Label (ACL) | 1961 One-Way Bottle (OWB) | 1975 One-Way Bottle (Plastic)

Compelling Journey

30

The mass of men lead lives of quiet desperation—
David Henry Thoreau

FROM TINY ACORNS 1941

The sapling at our house in Naples in 1941 grew to enormous size. A storm blew it over, and it crushed the house.

Earl Stubbs

It didn't take long for Mama to get her fill of the icehouse engagement in Mt. Pleasant. After a few months, we moved east eighteen miles to Naples. The family had lived there before my time, and the bustling town had some advantages. It was closer to Flat Creek, where Grandpa Stubbs, Marvin, Uncle Carl, and Uncle Walter still lived on their farms. That was where the family discussions took place. Mama's husband, Uncle Dud Price, lived in company housing next to the Cotton Belt Railroad Bridge on the Sulphur River, which was a short distance away. However, I am not sure that the close proximity of Uncle Dud was a compelling factor in the move. His contribution to the family came mostly in the form of money.

It was Mama's pattern to fumigate a house before we moved in. She used two substances. According to current thinking, formaldehyde candles eradicated varmints, and sulfur candles exterminated germs. On the other hand, it could have been the other way around. I don't know how well the latter worked, but the varmint killer worked wonders. When we first walked into the house to look it over, the smell of rotting animal corpses in unreachable places knocked me to my knees. The stench wasn't much better when we moved in a week later, and the worst odor was in the kitchen where we ate.

Compelling Journey

Three trees out front guarded the house. One was the largest magnolia tree I had ever observed. Another was a Chinaberry tree on its last leg. A portion of the tree flourished, while the other part was a large dead trunk. It stood perilously close to the storm cellar door. The third tree was a pin oak sapling about twelve feet tall. All three of these trees gained notoriety in their own way.

The Magnolia was my favorite. When we first arrived, I could not quite attain a handhold that would allow me to reach the large, lower branches and climb the tree. It took awhile, but, before the summer passed, I finally did so, surveyed my domain from the upper reaches. Over the proceeding months and years, I made a seat about halfway to the top, killed lots of Japs and Germans from hiding, and peppered passing cars with my BB gun.

The Chinaberry tree provided ammunition for our rock shooters. Its location near the storm cellar door was unfortunate. Often, if it thundered a couple of times, nervous neighbors crowded into our underground refuge fearing the worst. This could happen at any time of the day or night.

One morning, during the wee hours, we actually had a thunderstorm, and the wind blew down the dead portion of the Chinaberry tree onto the cellar door. When the storm abated, and we attempted to extricate ourselves from this haven of safety, the door would not budge. After sunup, passersby noted the dilemma and removed the tree. To prevent another such incident, the men folk cut down the live portion of the tree as well. The personality of our front yard changed and so did a source of ammunition for our slings.

To justify rising from a sound sleep during the middle of the night to go into a storm cellar shared with snakes and black widow spiders, Mama often stated, "A cyclone is going to come and blow us all away." She proved prophetic. As the decades passed, the sapling gained the stature of a giant. It must have been five feet in diameter and could have been the model for the beanstalk Jack climbed. Sure enough in 2008, a thunderstorm spawned a powerful wind that blew down the huge tree directly onto my childhood home and crushed it. Mama was right. It just took a few decades for her prophecy to come true.

Our home in Naples was the second house on the east side of the Daingerfield highway across the railroad tracks from downtown Naples. Yes, once again, we lived on the wrong side of the tracks. The property had a nice, empty lot on the north side, a pasture on the east side, and another lot on the south side. A barn, suitable for cows, hay, feed, and our car, sat on the southeast corner. We had running water in the form of two faucets: one outside for the animals and one in the kitchen for us humans. Our former two houses had bathrooms. This one did not. Using the outhouse was challenging, especially during inclement weather, and a slop jar even more so. The sounds of humans performing bodily functions became a normal, albeit unwelcome, part of our lives.

We had a small closet in the sleeping porch. When forced by conditions to use a pot, I used the cabinet for privacy. Once, I found myself mounted on the utensil when visitors arrived. Everyone congregated in the sleeping porch. What would it look like for a nine-year-old boy to come slinking out of a closet? Everyone would know. After I waited about thirty minutes, I swallowed my pride and came out. Mama didn't help when she announced, "Bud's been using the pot."

There was no natural gas hooked up to our house at that time. The women used a wood cook stove that required pine kindling and stove wood. The fireplace in a front room was the only other source of heat. We used hardwood in the fireplace, because it lasted longer and burned hotter. If I slept in any of the other three bedrooms during the winter, I got toasty warm at the fireplace and dashed for my icy bed. Jumping under the thick piles of cotton quilts; I suffered until body heat provided a warm cocoon for the night. The fetal position was the most common method for fighting the cold.

We did have electricity. Single bulbs hung from the ceilings of each room with a string to turn it off and on. Ellie had a little green fan, which she kept for herself during the stifling summer heat. I still have the fan, and it operates smoothly.

We didn't have a living room as such. Most of the house rooms held beds, except the dining room, the kitchen, and a small, narrow storeroom, which became my place of refuge. The main social gathering place during winter was in the bedroom with the fireplace. It contained two double beds, a couple of straight-backed chairs, and Mama's rocker, which was the only chair to have a cushion.

An biannual migration took place in our house according to the time of year, and the perceived needs of Mama. The summer gathering place was the sleeping porch. It was an add-on room at the back of the house surrounded by windows. If there was a breeze during the summer, it was the most comfortable place for resting and sleeping. Mama did a lot of both.

On the south side of our property was a patch of cane-like plants. They made great spears with which to emulate characters in the movies. My first friend after we moved to Naples was a black boy who passed by our

Compelling Journey

house quite often. Not knowing anything about racial prejudice at that time, Junior and I struck up a friendship. We threw spears and played games right up until the time Mama spotted my playmate. She came storming out of the house and ordered Junior to leave and not come back. I was bewildered and still am.

My next playmate was a large boy named A.J. Wells. He began hanging out at our house, and we spent some time playing together. One day, he got rough with me. Mama proceeded to visit with his mother and suggest that A.J. play with someone else. He didn't come back.

In 1941, we settled down in the house on Daingerfield Street for the next twelve years. My home place improved as the years passed. We got natural gas, a nice gas cook stove, and space heaters for the other bedrooms. For a small increase in the rent, our property owner added a bathroom. The icebox lost out to a refrigerator, and the wash pot to a washing machine.

For as long as it lasted, I viewed the house on Daingerfield Street as home, just as I do the town of Naples. I still visit the area a couple of times each year to get a hometown fix even though the house is no longer there. There is always someone in the local diner who can discuss old times.

Earl Stubbs

EARLY NAPLES

Compelling Journey

31

The very aim and end of our institutions is just this: that we may think what we like and say what we think--Oliver Wendell Holmes Sr.

CROSS-EYED NATIVES
1942

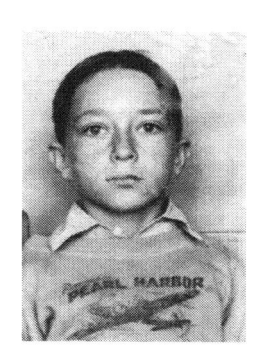

Age 7

Earl Stubbs

When August of 1941 completed the unrecognizable change to September, I launched my second attempt at a formal education by enrolling in the first grade of the Naples Grade School. My teacher, Ms. Gladys Martin, was the same person who taught Ellie, my foster-sister/cousin, some twenty-six years previously. The orange brick building was the same as well. It nestled atop the highest point in northern Morris County and held classes one through eight. Mrs. Martin's room was on the northeast corner of the ground floor.

After the excitement of going to school for the first time in several months, participating in the early morning lineup, and marching to class after the electric bell sounded, I found my assigned seat. The first day did not run smoothly. Students became lost. The quarterback of our future football team refused to turn loose of his mother's hand.

We observed our classmates and formed opinions about our own clothing and school supplies. One fashion conscious young lady wore dresses from Neiman-Marcus. Other less than trendy apparel lagged far behind the fashion times. My overalls were examples of the latter. My school supplies included a single row box of crayons. The high rollers had boxes with two or three rows. Some students had notebooks. Oh my! I had a Big Chief Tablet. The shame of it all.

Compelling Journey

When Mrs. Martin took command and launched our formal education, my VIP status emerged. She asked for a show of hands as to whether or not we could read, knew our numbers, and could print our names, and my hand shot up each time. After I breezed through Dick and Jane, a star was born albeit only briefly. It took about a month for the cream to rise to the top and for me to assume my mediocre but rightful position in the academic hierarchy of the class.

**Naples Grade School
1886 - 1951**

Destiny required that I spend the next twelve years with the majority of my classmates. Many of the bonds formed in Mrs. Martin's class endure to the present time.

Earl Stubbs

My association with classmates never ceased to be an important part of my existence. I suspect that my starvation for playmates during my early years influenced me in that direction. Paulette Coker, Don Dawson, Bill Hampton, Geneva Higgins, Jack Harvey, Peggy McNatt, Don Nance, Bobby Presley, Randall Raines, Tommy Walls, A. J. Wells, and Billy Williams began together in 1941, and we graduated together in 1953.

My social education developed on the playground, which had a dearth of equipment, since the Great Depression was still in full swing. There were swings, a seesaw, a carousel made from steel pipes, monkey bars, and a set of chinning bars. There were three levels to the latter apparatus, and the first graders used the lowest bar. It was the only one I could jump up and grab.

Within a few days, I had a pal. He was tall, skinny, and had a shock of thick, black hair. His name was Donald Ray Dawson. We gravitated to each other at recess and became best playground friends. Donald went home on the bus after school. I walked home down the long hill to town, across the railroad tracks, and along the Daingerfield highway to the second house on the left.

Across the street from my home was a large two-story apartment house. Four families lived there. Climbing

Compelling Journey

the magnolia tree one Saturday, I was astonished to see my good friend Donald saunter across the street. He had moved into the apartment house. Fate delivered my playmate for life right next door. We traveled through childhood, the teen years, and to the present time as the best of friends. Our adventures would fill numerous volumes. We are more like siblings than friends are, because I can still get angrier with my good friend Donald than I can with anyone else, especially when he beats me at gin. He cheats. I know he cheats. After sixty years of playing, I just can't determine how he does it.

The first grade group of students provided my first true love. Her name was Shirley McCoy. Like her namesake, Shirley Temple, a mass of curls adorned her lovely head. She was the smartest member of our class, and to rub it in, she was drop-dead gorgeous. She had a charming, gap-toothed smile and wore little fur-topped boots with a pocket for a knife. She had it all. My heart broke when she did not return to school for the second grade, and she dropped off the face of the earth. I can only assume that she went back to heaven.

A few weeks after the beginning of school, a true legend enrolled in our class. His name was Jack Harvey. During the entirety of our time together, Jack ruled. He

Earl Stubbs

was funny, smarter than the rest of us, beloved by his teachers, and everyone who knew him. He never cut up in class or got into trouble. He attended church, did not smoke, and grew into a tall, handsome athlete. Jack was most popular, most handsome, and chosen for leadership for the duration of our twelve years together. I still, respectfully, refer to him as The Legend. To this day, we manage to visit at least once each year, even though he lives in the Houston area, and a bit of his enamel cracked over the years.

There were two versions of Shirley Temple in the class. Another was Paulette Coker. Early on, while I still had some status in the room, she chose me to escort her during the Halloween Carnival. I was elated to do so. After Shirley ascended, Paulette became the undisputed queen and social director of our class.

A. J. went to school the year before, but Mrs. Martin deemed that he needed a firmer foundation. His father died during this time, and his difficult life became more challenging. We had many laughs and got into much trouble making faces at one another during class.

Though I wouldn't know it for many decades, I dealt with attention deficit disorder. Managing down time in class was not my strong suit, so I found myself in Dutch with teachers for the duration of my public school time. Though Mrs. Martin was a reticent, no-nonsense kind of educator, we maintained our friendship until her death years later. I can say that only about one other of my teachers.

The Naples schools had no cafeterias. Most students brought a brown paper sack lunch. Peanut butter and jelly sandwiches were at the bottom of the social and culinary ladder. Money mattered come lunchtime, unless one had special circumstances. I did. Ellie worked at Joe's Café slinging hash or waiting tables to be more exact. For the grand total of twenty-five cents per day, I could eat like a king. My lunch fare included a hamburger, a coke, and a double-dip cream cone.

I learned from my classmates that I was the only one who did not attend the Saturday western matinee at the Inez Theater. Asking Mama to part with hard money for something as frivolous as going to the movies was akin to asking her to pull out a tooth and give it to me. To say that Mama was frugal is like saying the Pacific Ocean is wet. After months of nagging on my part, Mama finally began parting with the nine cents for the Saturday movie. Each time she parted with the dime, she demanded that I bring home the change.

In the movies, heroes remained in constant conflict with natives, who were whatever spear chunking, arrow shooting, and sparsely dressed people the movie script needed for a corpse-littered battlefield. They died by the thousands due to their poor weapons and propensity to charge blazing guns. Natives were fair game.

During the fits of imagination that overcame my concentration while my classmates engaged in schoolwork, I invented the cross-eyed natives. As the legend grew, my perceived sect was quite normal except for their eye problem. They saw two of everything. To compound matters, they lived in tree houses, so in order to enter their houses; they had to determine which of the two ladders was real. In most instances, they chose the wrong one and went sprawling. The problem was worse when they climbed down.

My creations were inept at warfare. After all, they had to choose the correct target for their spears, so they missed at least fifty-percent of the time. They could not run through the forest with impunity, because they were always picking the wrong tree and smashing into the real one. They had the same problem with cooking, finding food, and threading a needle. On more than one occasion, Mrs. Martin succumbed to class pressure and turned the class over to me. I would spin cross-eyed native tales on the fly. Even today, every time Jack Harvey and I get together, we have a laugh at their expense.

Compelling Journey

**Naples High School
1926 - 1951**

Earl Stubbs

32

The hole and the patch should be commensurate—Thomas Jefferson

Este es el Gato
1943

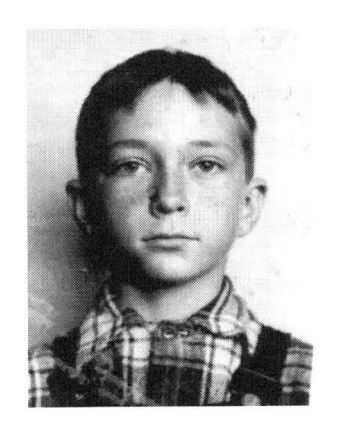

Age 9

Compelling Journey

The second and third years at the Naples Grade School made fewer lasting impressions, however, there are several worth recording for posterity. I recall the second grade in terms of a dark room and the color clash between a red sweater and pink undergarments.

Our second grade teacher, unlike Mrs. Martin, was a buxom young woman. My behavior patterns being what they were, I drew her ire on more than one occasion each day. She rarely approved of my need to help direct activities, especially in the area of comedy, so there you are. As strange as it sounds, I wanted her affection and approval just as much as the good kids, but I couldn't make that happen. However, I knew when to curtail the fun and games. I never received a lick from any teacher during all of my years in school...except for Coach Ramey and his broom which doesn't count.

Our teacher favored red sweaters. I don't know if the weave was looser during the war years, but her sweater reminded me of a fish net covering her more than ample bosoms and pink undergarments. Apparently, she had a large supply of these articles of clothing, because she wore a red sweater almost every day. At the very least, her fashion choices provided a focal point for the boys' attention, when we were not engrossed in our studies.

Earl Stubbs

My third grade teacher was Miss Hazel Rice. She was tall, slim, and had a good disposition. I recall her as a very good teacher, who managed me without losing her temper. She created unusual lerning projects to keep our interest. One of her most successful forays was to teach us a few words in Spanish. Este es el gato was the first sentence. This translates to *this is the cat*. After we mastered the first sentence, Miss Rice gave us el gato de bebidas de leche. *The cat drinks milk*. She provided el perro, *the dog*, next, etc. Those class exercises indelibly seared those few words of Spanish into my memory banks. Unfortunately, Miss Rice soon ran out of Spanish. We could have easily learned the entire language, but there was no money for a Spanish teacher. If I had learned the parts of English speech and their application as well that school year, my first semester at ET would not have included English 111X Or Idiot English, as we liked to call it.

Having lost Shirley McCoy after the first grade, and having Paulette Coker move on to more physically impressive boys, I was in dire need of a girl to moon over. The third grade provided Ouida Hampton. She was a dark-eyed beauty who captivated her classmates with her brilliance and charm. She would become the valedictorian of our graduating class, and in the early years, aptitude in class equaled respect and popularity.

Compelling Journey

Even though I didn't say two words to Ouida all year, she was never far from my thoughts.

My academic patterns established themselves during these years and remained unchanged through high school. My teachers described me as an A student who made B's. I was already better educated than either Mama or Uncle Dud, so there was no one to provide the guidance needed to develop study habits and complete homework. I was unaware of the correlations between behavior patterns in class and grades, between family social status in the community and grades, and between teacher attitudes and grades as well. It was only after the completion of my education that I discovered those dynamic patterns, not that it would have mattered. We are what and who we are.

I don't know much about plumbing, but the water pressure at the Naples Grade School was geared to coincide with the outside temperature. The hotter and drier the temperature, the slower and warmer the water ran. On those blistering September and May days, after running hard for the duration of recess, our mouths were bone dry and our need for water overwhelming. During such times, the water virtually dribbled out of the fountains, much to the dismay of the wilting students in the long lines waiting to drink. I never could understand why the fountains ran so freely during winter and so poorly when it was hot.

Keep in mind that this was an ancient building constructed considerably before the turn of the twentieth century. Water pressure at the fountains was not the only plumbing problem. It seemed that the sewage pipes were always stopped up, and the pungent odor life threatening. However, considering the state of the world's economy at the time, we were fortunate to have a restroom at all. It was better than what I had at home.

Smoking was commonplace among children during those times. I vividly recall the acrid taste from the puffs on my first cigarette. I was five and we sat at the kitchen table of the house by the tracks in Mt. Pleasant.

Even though my family members encouraged me to use tobacco, I did not smoke at school. I only smoked a few times a week at that time. I had my own pack by the age of ten. Cigarettes were cheap, especially if you could roll your own, and medical science had made no correlation between tobacco and health.

I smoked when I was bored or could not get out of the house. Over the years, the addiction grew, and I would smoke for forty-five long years before finally breaking the habit. Smoking had a profound affect on my life. I refused an athletic scholarship to ET, because I knew I could not stop smoking. By that time, tobacco had

Compelling Journey

already damaged my lungs and flawed my endurance. I have not smoked in twenty-four years, but I am as addicted to nicotine as ever.

Even though a single bulb hanging from the ceiling lighted all of my grade school rooms, I recollect my different classrooms in terms of light. Light filled my first grade room. My second grade room was dark with no fellow students standing out with the exception of A.J. Wells making faces. The third grade room was dark, but some students and teachers seem to glow in my memories. Of course, some rooms had more windows than others, and that may have been a factor.

Don Dawson continued to share my time on the playground and at home. Our pattern was to close out the day outside if the weather was nice. We found other things to do on our own in winter. For all of the thousands of hours we spent playing together during our years growing up, we spent very little playtime inside the houses. Neither of us felt very comfortable in the other's house. I really don't know what Don did, but I created battles with marauding cowboys, Indians, Germans, and Japs, and fought them off with my silver six-shooter and whatever other weapon I could find. My mode of transportation was the arm of Mama's rocking chair, which served as my horse. My sound effects were magnificent. Of course, all activity came to a halt whenever another family member entered the room.

Compelling Journey

33

A banker is a fellow who lends you his umbrella when the sun is shining, but wants it back the minute it begins to rain...Mark Twain

THE CRIME SPREE
1945

I will never escape the lessons of the fourth grade, nor would I wish to. One of the brief human candles that flared during my formative years sputtered to life once again just last week. Wayne Raney, a refugee from Shreveport, joined our class in 1944 and quickly became the leader of the gang. Wayne wore his blond hair carefully combed, starched, khaki shirt sleeves rolled up twice, and a stiff collar raised in the back. He didn't walk; he strutted. He was the favorite of the girls, and his practical knowledge was peerless, so why not?

Wayne taught us many things, including all of the relevant cuss words, which we practiced with great regularity. It took a while before I realized that God would not strike us dead if we uttered the words where He could hear them. Wayne named the reproductive parts of both male and female anatomy with terms we had never heard. He discussed the sexual habits of humans on a constant basis with both expertise and color.

To my utter surprise, he wrote me a letter last week wanting to purchase my recent novel. He lives in California but must still have relatives in northeast Texas, since I advertise in the Naples Monitor each week. I spoke with him only once since 1945. When Wayne visited a class reunion several years ago, he had maintained his charm and good looks albeit in an undersized package.

The fourth grade produced numerous events and people who still crowd my recollections. Several of the people came and went, but their presence made a permanent impression. Hershel "Sweetpea" Welch and Ben Grimes joined us for that year and then returned to James Bowie, a school across the Sulfur River from Naples. Patsy Green came on board, and we spent time laughing and talking when we should have been working.

The fourth grade was the first year that we played organized games. In the past, we spent our recess time on the swings, monkey bars, etc. During the fourth

Compelling Journey

grade, Mrs. Exa Tolbert, one of my favorite teachers, introduced us to softball. While our designated playground area did not lend itself to a ball field, we made do with what we had. Chunks of concrete served as bases. The space allowed barely enough room for the diamond, so when our heavy hitters connected, the ball sailed over the Agriculture classroom or the gym or occasionally through a window. I learned that if I pulled the ball near third base, it would go down a steep hill, and I could get my share of home runs.

Mrs. Exa taught us the game and supervised our play. When the Bell rang for recess, we all started screaming for the positions we wanted. Someone, usually A. J. Wells, would yell, "First batter!" Then someone else would scream, "First batter," after which A. J. would shout, "I said first." And so on. Meanwhile, the student who arrived first and grabbed the bat seldom gave it up. First batter was the plum, then second batter, third, pitcher, first base, and so on. Coy Moreland was everyone's favorite pitcher, because he served up fat ones. During play, if someone caught a fly, he immediately assumed the place of the hitter.

This was the first time I had an opportunity to use any athletic ability I might or might not possess. I had to learn to catch the ball in my small hands. I watched the

Earl Stubbs

other boys carefully. Dane Shaw had a baseball family, and he already knew how to catch. I patterned my technique after Dane. Those days throwing the old tennis ball against the chimney in Mt. Pleasant helped immensely. I had to learn to hit the ball. Jack Harvey batted cross-handed, but he was the best hitter with A. J. a close second. I soon learned that I did games well enough, and a future jock flourished. I never lost the thrill of victory nor the agony of defeat as described during later years on the Wild World of Sports.

Mrs. Exa was a resourceful classroom teacher as well. She was firm, and that took some adjustments on my part. I recall the study of grammar and history. Did we learn our multiplication tables that year? I believe we did. I recall the room as well lighted, and I can see my fellow students clearly. That means that it was a good year.

The most memorable event during the fourth grade began with our occasional classmate, Alvis Donald "Sunshine" Franklin. Since he did not spend very much time in school, Sunshine had time on his hands, and he spent some of it scouting out opportunities. One thing he learned was that a front window of the grade school was unlocked most of the time, and we all knew that the ice cream box and cold drink boxes were unlocked as well.

Compelling Journey

Sunshine made a few forays into the building and helped himself to the goodies therein. Since our gang did not always have specific plans after the Saturday matinee at the Inez Theater, we chose to join Sunshine on his next escapade. Four or five of us climbed through the unlocked window and raided the ice cream and drink coolers. What could be better?

It turned out to be the perfect crime, but by the next week, the word was out that hardened criminals were breaking into the grade school and stealing valuable property. We gulped at the news and went about our business.

Back to the international scene. The war was winding down. The war in Europe demonstrated the victory of right over wrong. Patton and the Russians ran amok in Europe. US troops under McArthur and Nimitz reclaimed Pacific islands in preparation for the invasion of the Japanese homeland. However, due to his health issues, President F. D. Roosevelt succumbed on 12 April 1945. That was a Saturday, and we made the poor choice of heading for the grade school to obtain some illicit refreshments. Bad choice.

After eating and drinking our fill, a few gang members put extra drinks in their pockets, and we left the building. We were eating and drinking our way down the hill behind the school, when a pair of riders appeared. Just like in the westerns. One was Bobby Godsey, the constable's son. The other was Thomas Harvey, the blacksmith's son, and brother of my classmate Jack.

For some unknown reason, a couple of the boys panicked and started running. To make matters worse, they began throwing soft drink bottles. The riders pursued us out of curiosity. Thomas was a smart person. When he saw the drink bottles flying, he knew what they had discovered. They had serendipitously exposed the heart and soul of the crime wave that had ravished the school for the last month. Thomas and Bobby ratted us out.

I was petrified. I raced home and hid in my book room, but to no avail. Soon, Constable Godsey knocked on the front door. The constable had a marked resemblance to Boris Karloff of Frankenstein fame. The man looked dead when he was alive. Think Frankenstein's monster in a Stetson hat.

He asked to see Mama, and I complied. After he left, Mama laid out the plea bargain. I was to pay my share of the cost of the stolen goods while visiting Superintendent Wommack's office the next Monday. I might or might not get licks. I knew that if I did, they would result in my death. The final stipulation was that if I ever, in my entire life, took anything that did not belong to me, Mr.

Compelling Journey

Godsey would immediately pick me up and deliver me to reform school, a fate even worse than passing away. I immediately became a Christian, at least temporarily. I am sure that if I stole something at this late date in my life, Constable Godsey would come out of the grave and take me away.

The following Monday was the real day of infamy. Sweat poured off my brow all day until the summons came. Superintendent of Schools Wommack was a big man with wiry gray hair. He knew my family, when we were a family, so he did not pass up the opportunity to tell me that my sisters would be very disappointed in my behavior. That broke my heart, but it quickly repaired itself when he allowed me to leave without the dreaded licks. I suggest that mumbling the Lord's Prayer under my breath during this ordeal may have swayed the outcome. Some members of our band, including Sunshine and A.J., without such political influence were not so fortunate. Fairness did not always blend into the politics of the time.

Earl Stubbs

34

The place where optimism most flourishes is the lunatic asylum--<u>Havelock Ellis</u>

Age 11

HOLD THE PRESSES
1946

The fifth grade room was light and airy. It was on the second floor at the back of the grade school building. The biggest surprise of the year was the first day when we

Compelling Journey

met Miss Grisham. She was an eighteen-year-old, movie star blond in a petite body. Glamour was a big word in those days, and she had a ton.

The word on the street was that she was the fiancée of a wealthy local boy, who may have served in the armed forces at the time. Whatever the real story, Miss Grisham delighted us for one school year, and then she moved on without her affluent prospect. Something tells me she had no problem in obtaining a replacement down the road.

Several of my classmates from the fourth grade left before school began. Ben Grimes, Hershel Welch, and Wayne Raney departed for greener pastures. However, the solid core of our class remained. Don Dawson and I still ran the streets together. Jack Harvey was everyone's favorite. Paulette and Ouida were the prettiest and smartest and academics became more fun. That was because of Miss Grisham.

This was her first teaching job, and she exuded enthusiasm. Like Miss Rice, she came up with an abundance of neat classroom projects. Most of the special ventures required student leadership, and guess who was never selected to serve? No matter how many times I volunteered my services, my success rate was nil. I must admit that Miss Grisham's classroom activities

Earl Stubbs

were stimulating, so my ADD personality was most often in high gear. I may not have been one of her favorites.

As my frustration level grew, I came up with a scheme. I suggested to Miss Grisham that we needed a class newspaper, and I would volunteer to be the editor. The class had some other activities underway at the time, or I could have made the suggestion during the middle of math class, but she turned my inspiration aside. Undeterred, I brought the suggestion up on several other occasions even though I could perceive when she became irritated with my persistence. Finally, after one of my sojourns into the subject, she said, "Fine. We will have a class newspaper, and you can be the editor. Now what would you like to do?"

What would I like to do? That was not part of the plan. Miss Grisham's role was to plan our activities, tell us all what to do, and I would have my name on the banner. Editors don't really have to really do anything...Do they?

She was insistent. She gave me one special assignment, which was to bring a plan for the class newspaper the next day...No excuses. Even the last recess of the day was not fun.

After school, I dragged myself home, went to my book room, and applied myself to the project. The first thing I did was to write an editorial about how important class

Compelling Journey

leaders, such as editors, should be first at bat during recess. Next, I decided to bend the big-time operators in class to my will and force them to do the actual work. I assigned articles to the best students. When I went to bed that night, my nervous system had settled itself to a degree.

Since this was an English project, I had to contain myself during the morning classes, recess, and lunch, but the time arrived when Miss Grisham called upon me to present my plan for a class newspaper. I strolled to the front of the room and laid out how a much needed classroom project would unfold. I notified my chosen reporters that we had a deadline, and that they had two days to provide me with their assigned articles. When I finished, to an absence of applause, Miss Grisham picked out one of the chosen reporters and asked her if she wanted to be on the class newspaper staff. She said no. The teacher went through the list of my reporters, and they all declined. Then Miss Grisham turned to me and said, "Mr. Editor, you have one week to complete our paper. What will you do next?"

Recess that day was not much fun either. I decided that I might have to lower my standards when selecting my reporters.

Earl Stubbs

Before the next day was over, my knees were dirty because I had spent so much time on them begging classmates to write an article for the class paper. Those that actually agreed to do so wanted me to provide the subject and most of the prose. It was a struggle, but by the deadline, we put together enough verbiage to fill both sides of a single sheet of paper. True to her word, Miss Grisham ran off copies on the mimeograph, and we all had a copy of our first class newspaper. Each reporter got to read their own contribution aloud. Truth be known, several of the copies of the paper were reduced to airplanes before the readings concluded.

When the final reader uttered the last word, Miss Grisham asked me in a pleasant tone, "Well Mr. Editor, what do you have in mind for next week?"

I may be slow, but I am not stupid. I answered, "Maybe someone else could be editor next week?" She smiled and said nothing further about class newspapers. I learned to live without positions of leadership and everyone profited.

Compelling Journey

35

Those who are really in earnest must be willing to be anything or nothing in the world's estimation—Susan B. Anthony

Age 13

SATURDAY IN NAPLES
1946

Earl Stubbs

When I visit Naples and take my drive up past the water tower, I attempt to equate the overgrown vacant lot to our ancient school buildings full of noisy children.

A quiet East Texas town surrounds the area. It's mostly a bedroom community with its inhabitants working all over Northeast Texas. Naples appears clean even with some of the main street buildings boarded up. The new world of Interstate Highways, TV's, and Wal-Marts left many such small towns behind. As a matter of course, town businesses, and the merchants who ran them, went the way of the farmer. However, the town I committed to memory during the 1940's was something entirely different especially on a Saturday. It was noisy, colorful, and odors permeated the air, sometimes pleasant, sometimes not. Smells told of giant steam engines and the wet coats of free running dogs. They spoke of hot popcorn, spent spring showers, and passing livestock and their residue. They spoke of freshly mown lawns and chicken fried steaks, if one was near the City Café, or moist hamburgers and coconut cream pie if one was near Joe's Cafe on the other end of town. I can close my eyes, take in some of the clean air, and paint a picture of life in the Naples of my childhood.

Even the colors seemed brighter--especially the variety on the advertisements in front of the Inez Theater depicting coming attractions. On the streets of Naples,

Compelling Journey

women wore bright cotton frocks often accented with radiant head scarves and wide belts. Both men and women wore hats. In the summer, straw hats were the order of the day. In the winter, men wore impressive felt hats with snap brims. Strangely enough, only the men who worked cattle wore cowboy style hats. A few wore Stetsons, but not nearly as many as today. The skies exuded blue, the lawns oozed green, and trees radiated fall colors more impressive to the eyes of a child. It was as if God decreed that clouds and bad weather were not welcome in Naples on a Saturday.

Sounds permeated the air including runaway herds of cattle emanated from the Inez Theater. No Saturday movie was complete without stampeding cattle, numerous fist fights, and countless shootouts. A few songs and some slapstick were thrown in for good measure. They were all on the silver screen. The horns of automobiles often accented the noisy atmosphere. The toot of a horn was considered a form of greeting. Heavy trucks rumbled Northeast and Southwest on Highway 67, competing with the endless rattle of freight and passenger trains. Soldiers shouted in strange accents from troop trains, as they directed us kids to bring them cokes and cigarettes while the train was on a siding. I wonder how many lived and how many died. We heard

Earl Stubbs

countless people in conversation on the streets, and we could mostly recognize the person just from the sound of their voices. We heard small children squealing as they raced from one end of town to the other, their safety assured.

No air conditioning existed in either automobiles, homes, or in town. Even during the dog days of summer, only the shade of awnings alleviated the heat. In the places of business, the whir of countless electric fans moved the air and afforded patrons a small measure of relief. The only time I noticed the high temperature was when I walked on the burning sidewalks or highways.

The Naples I knew and loved is gone. The world and my town evolved since I moved away in 1953 to the extent that little bares a resemblance to the past. I did not witness the transformation which marks the changes even more noticeably. Naples of sixty years ago was a vibrant, busy place whose inhabitants had a lot at stake. However, not all was peace and light. The wolf was much closer to the door in those days and adults were a serious albeit fun loving lot. Poverty-stricken people still lived in Morris County during the 1940's. Some went to bed hungry with several sharing a room and sometimes a bed. We did not all enjoy the latest styles in our wardrobes. Thirty-five cents per hour was the going

Compelling Journey

wage around town, and one had to work long and hard to earn enough money to make a difference.

I have no way of knowing how well the local merchants were doing in those days, but there were a lot of them. I do know that they stayed open long hours, and that in some cases, the competition was fierce. The stakes were high. The town supported three major grocery stores and several minor ones. There was a movie house, a dry goods store, a five and dime, a barber shop, a bus station, a train station, two major automobile dealerships complete with repair facilities, a thriving newspaper, a cotton gin, seasonal produce including watermelons and cucumbers, three drugstores, a solid bank, numerous eating establishments, a dry cleaners, numerous gas stations, a physician, a dentist, a lawman, an auto supply store, a public restroom, and on a couple of occasions a summer snow-cone stand operated by entrepreneur Don Nance. I can count one high school student who drove his own car and it was a Model A Ford....I think. There was no little league but lots of games underway. The most important days of the week for me and my contemporaries, were Friday, Saturday, and Sunday. Friday was important, because school was out for the week, and one could look forward to Saturday. Saturday was exceptional because it was so exciting from 7 a.m. until 1 a.m. on Sunday. Sunday was extraordinary, because it was truly a day of rest that included church services and maybe an afternoon movie at the Inez Theater.

On Saturday people from the surrounding area descended on Naples with whatever money or credit they had in order to buy food and supplies for the week. Citizens arranged transportation if they had none of their own, purchased whatever they needed or could afford, and then just roamed the streets watching others or visiting with acquaintances. People on the move virtually choked the street from one end to the other. A coke was a treat, and none of us knew that it was laced with caffeine. A burger cost $.25, but it would take two to equal a normal burger today. Patrons filled the Inez theater to overflowing from the time it opened until it closed at 1:00 a.m. Parents went about the events of the day and left children to look out for themselves. That meant that kids were racing from one end of the street to the other and from store to store. Most of the adults knew them by sight and accepted them as a part of the landscape. The children spoke to adults when they met one they knew by name, and there was interest between the two.

Highway 67 was a major transportation and commercial artery that ran through Our town, and

Compelling Journey

eighteen wheelers rolled through the city during all hours. Crossing the highway was not taken lightly. Freight and passenger trains rumbled through moving the nations goods across the country. One could take a Cotton Belt train or Greyhound bus ride to Texarkana and points east or to Dallas and points west. Few people in Naples at that time had ever seen an airplane on the ground and only a very few had ever flown in one. Occasionally, a mule drawn wagon creaked down the street and parked behind the buildings.

The major sources of entertainment were radio shows and movies. I became familiar with radio voices rather than the faces of movie stars. Examples were Laraine Tuttle and Dashell Hammet. Soap operas such as Young Widow Brown ran during the day along with music by the Light Crust Doughboys from Burrus Mills. After listening to a flour commercial, one would have thought that a Light Crust biscuit could cure cancer. W. Leo Daniel became governor of Texas by using the radio to reach voters and promising outlandish pensions to the old folks should he be elected and he was. Names like Red Skelton and Jack Benny became known all over the country. The Shadow, the Green Hornet, and Mr. District Attorney fought crime and always won. Radio was available to most and children re-enacted their favorite programs at school the next day. Edward R. Murrow reported national and world news in his distinctive style. The children of my generation listened to the reality of war news and the unreality of radio and movie heroes. The focus of the nation postponed school athletics until after the war.

Was the Naples of the 1940's a better place? That is a question that can never be answered. Ignorance was more pervasive. Little real crime came to our attention other than a constable shooting up a neighborhood doing his duty. People were out and about, and as a result, spent more time together. A social error such as a pregnancy destroyed lives and rarely came to light. The cast system was real and in place. Rock hard racism flourished. A white child playing with a black child, except for exchanging stones in a rock fight, was not allowed.

When I moved to Naples in 1941, I began playing with a young black boy named Junior. We had such a wonderful time until the grownups involved themselves. Junior would be about eighty by now, and I hope he flourishes. I always got a howdy from Miss Veenie and her sons Jack and Red. Some of us followed our own instincts where other folks were concerned. Most did not. It was a town, much like most of the Southern USA, segregated by thoughts and deeds.

Compelling Journey

At present, one cannot find a similar way of life in small towns or even large towns for that matter. There is little reason for people to get out of their air-conditioned houses on a regular basis and intermingle. Maybe it exists in developing third world countries, where citizens still rub elbows, but not in this country. Will it ever return? Not likely. People have too many reasons to stay at home.

The witnesses of life in Naples of sixty years ago are showing the signs of age. Some of us are not the healthiest people on the planet, and many of us are not here anymore. How can we be so near the end of our time and have so few answers? Before too many more years, the memories of the vibrant Naples of our youth will pass with us, and the noisy, bustling place of the fabulous forties will cease to be even a memory. It was something special. Considering the times, the people, modern conveniences, the rearing of children, the kindred spirits, and the opportunities, if I could roll back the clock and design my own hometown, I wouldn't change a thing.

Earl Stubbs

36

It is better that some should be unhappy, than none should be happy, which would be the case in a general state of equality—Samuel Johnson

THE GREAT LUMBERYARD FIGHT 1947

It is unfortunate, but fighting among boys was not uncommon while growing up in Northeast Texas. One of the things you knew about your schoolmates was whether or not you could whip them. Most of us let our brains do our fighting, and we made those determinations without actually testing the waters. Since I couldn't whip very many people and had almost no enemies, I always served as a willing spectator. A classmate challenged me once, but I declined. In retrospect, I guess I should have gone ahead and taken my whipping, but the challenger was a good friend, and I really didn't want to win or lose to him.

There was almost no fighting at school in those days. If a disagreement became serious, the combatants would

Compelling Journey

arrange to meet at the old deserted courthouse after school with an audience. I believe the fights were more for entertainment than for blood, since they usually didn't last long and a bloody lip and a little sniffling was the usual result.

There were tough guys and victims. When challenges were levied, a tough guy called out someone he knew he could whip. The winner was always a forgone conclusion, and the process was most often according to script. The winner would throw a few punches, and finally, one would land. The loser would hit the ground and began to wail. At this point, I usually headed for home glad that it wasn't me doing the wailing.

There was one instance when two hefty lads of similar size and reputation, got into a disagreement at school and agreed to meet after school to settle the matter. Now both of these boys were tough, and the fight promised to be a battle royal. We could hardly wait until school was out, after which we marched en masse down to the courthouse. There were few preliminaries, both boys took their stance, and the fight began. Except it was all a big sham. Both boys began to dance around throwing fluffy punches that didn't land. It only took a few seconds for us to know that we were victims of a giant subterfuge. They had planned the whole thing, and we bit like hungry bass.

Without question though, the Bobby Mize and James Ed Alexander showdown was the best I ever saw. It was a real battle between two evenly matched opponents. You can have your Joe Lewis versus Billy Conn, your Sugar Ray Robinson verses Jake LaMotta, and even the Thrilla in Manilla. I'll put the Mize versus Alexander lumberyard brawl up against any of them. Even today, it would be worth the price of admission.

After World War II played out its violent and tragic end, people from all over the world left the armed forces, moved around, and started new lives. Naples, grew to the massive size of over 1,300 souls during this time. Veterans came home, joined their families, and carved out a slice of the Naples pie for themselves. I don't know the origin of the Mize family, but it was a rather large group by Naples standards and consisted of Mr. and Mrs. Mize, three sons, one of whom was Bobby Mize, and Betty, a member of my class. This was an interesting family, because their primary avocation was fist fighting.

The reference to fighting is a bit misleading. They were interested in boxing primarily, but occasionally, bare knuckles were okay as well. Goodness knows where we got our information, but we understood that Mr. Mize was a former professional boxer. The older boys were

Compelling Journey

also trained boxers, though I was not aware if they still pursued the sport at that point. I saw them wear boxing jackets...probably golden gloves. Even Betty knew a bit about fighting. Once on the playground, I teased her a bit too much and she responded with a hard, straight left to the point of my nose. I didn't tease Betty again.

Bobby was about fourteen or fifteen at the time and possessed all of the boxing knowledge passed down from his father and older brothers to go with an aggressive disposition. In addition to his knowledge of boxing, Bobby possessed a superb physique. He had broad heavy shoulders, massive biceps, a deep chest that narrowed down to slim hips, and strong legs. Bobby possessed the classic build for fighting. It was only natural that when he moved to town, he would look up the toughest kid and give him a go. That was James Ed Alexander.

James Ed had none of Bobby's training and exhibited none of his desire for fighting. He was just a rawboned kid with none of the muscle definition of Bobby. James Ed, and no one called him James or Ed, was a good athlete and a friendly person. It was common to speak to people around town in those days, and James Ed always spoke even though he was several years older. No one knew if he could fight or not, but he was a big kid with a rangy body. That was all that he needed to become a marked man. Bobby needed a sparing partner, and he elected James Ed.

Fights in Naples between the younger set occurred in one of two places. If the bout was an after school affair by grade school kids, they gathered at the courthouse. If it was a more serious affair between high school boys, which was rare, it most often happened in the lumberyard next door to the Inez Theater. This was one of the latter.

I don't know what preempted the challenge. When the boys I hung out with noticed the drama unfolding, the two combatants were standing in the lumberyard and were calmly discussing the rules of engagement. The primary discussion was whether the combatants would remove their rings. Bobby suggested that both boys remove their rings, and much to my surprise, James Ed indicated that he didn't care about rings. In the beginning, the rings stayed on.

I liked James Ed, but I didn't know Bobby very well. My impression, at the time, was that Bobby looked unbeatable, and that a good friend of mine was going to get himself worked over pretty good. I maintained that opinion until the fight was well under way.

The boys squared off, begun to probe each other, and the fighting personalities of both boys became apparent.

Compelling Journey

Bobby Mize demonstrated his skill and training in his basic stance and pugilistic affectations. He bounced up and down, feinted with both hands, and snorted loudly through his nose. James Ed stood in his naturally stooped posture, put up his hands, and waited. He didn't have to wait long. Bobby moved in and threw a series of quick punches that would have knocked off the heads of most people. To everyone's surprise, including Bobby, James Ed blocked several punches with his hands and moved his head to avoid the others. Incredibly, not a blow landed. However, that did not deter Bobby. He proceeded to initiate several other forays with pretty much the same results. He landed a few punches, but they were glancing blows, and for the most part, did no damage. James Ed was content to stay in his crouch and counter. After a bit, Bobby's rushing attacks became less demonstrative, and his snorts evolved into heavy breathing. James Ed did some evolving on his own. He began to throw a few more punches, and they were landing.

The bout slowly emerged into a ballet of sorts with both boys throwing and receiving punches. Bobby would initiate a series of punches, and James Ed would counterpunch with hard straight lefts and rights. He was, however, not using as much energy as Bobby, and the latter's flurries became less frequent. Those potent arms began to sag, and those powerful legs began to weaken. After a time, Bobby could barely lift his fists.

James Ed initiated his offense by well-placed left jabs that began to take a toll on Bobby's face. Then James Ed slipped a punch and delivered a hard right hand that surprised Bobby and all the members of the lumberyard audience. Bobby wiped his face and found blood on his hand. He stopped the fight, and requested that both boys take off their rings. James Ed complied, but the momentum still belonged to him. He moved forward and began using the hard left jab to keep Bobby worried. Then he would bring the straight right, and by this time, Bobby knew he was in trouble, but he never quit. Finally, James Ed threw a hard right to Bobby's jaw that put him on the ground. He didn't get up. The fight was over.

No one knew, least of all James Ed, but he was an extremely talented boxer. His slender body belied a powerful punch and hand quickness that would earn him a USN fleet championship in later years.

Bobby Mize didn't give up or stop fighting. He became a valued member of the Naples High School athletic program, especially the boxing team, and we were always glad to see him fighting for Naples High.

Compelling Journey

When Bobby fought, one way or the other, somebody went to sleep.

It is ironic that Bobby Mize and James Ed Alexander became the best of friends. They served as teammates on the athletic fields of Naples High School and served their country on the same ship during the Korean Conflict.

James Ed also boxed for the school and never lost a bout. He enjoyed great success as a Navy boxer and eventually we ended up at East Texas State Teachers College in the 50's as schoolmates once again. We picked up our friendship in college and enjoyed some great times. I can remember one incident when James Ed was asleep in his room at the Paragon House, and some people came in at 2 a.m. and dumped three crates of vegetables into his bed, but that's another story.

Earl Stubbs

37

**Lack of money is the root of all evil—
George Benard Shaw**

SMITH'S DRUG STORE
1949

Age 14

Compelling Journey

Two families provided the majority of the health care in Naples during the late 1930's and early 40's. Dr. Smith, a local family practice physician, delivered me into the world. His small, musty office was on the main street of Naples right next to Smith's Drug Store, owned and operated by his son, Wendell and daughter-in-law, Lois. Wendell's major competition was Leeve's Drug Store on the next block. Mr. Leeves was a pharmacist as well. He and his wife produced two sons, James and Jerry, who became physicians. James, or Jimmy as he was called, would spend his professional life practicing in Naples.

However, this story is not about health care but about an institution. Smith's Drug store was far more than just a pharmacy or a gift shop or a soda fountain or even a source for the latest in written media. It was the social gathering place at special times during the week and a major one on the weekends. One didn't just go to the movie on Sunday. One went to the movie and then stopped off at Smith's Drug Store for a Coke and a social interlude afterwards.

Whether by accident or by design, Smith's became a major part of growing up during the Naples experience of that era.

Earl Stubbs

When Smith's was open, and it was open most of the time, there was a steady stream of customers arriving, leaving, or just standing around the fountain sipping a quick Coke or indulging in the absolute best milkshakes maybe on the face of the earth. Following the Saturday or Sunday afternoon movie, I was usually faced with the decision of whether to spend my last 25 cents on one of those super milkshakes or purchase two comic books for a leisurely read at home. More often than not, the milkshake won out. It is ironic that a milkshake would alter forever my memories of Smith's Drugstore.

Smith's Drugstore was a well stocked gift shop and served as the town's primary source of reading material. Smith's carried a large stock of comic books, current newspapers from Dallas, Texarkana, and Shreveport plus an abundance of those wonderful magazines such as Life, Look, Colliers, and sports magazines as well.

Due to the large selection choosing a comic book was not a simple matter. The comics were on the bottom rack and one had to squat or sit on the floor to really sample the merchandise. There was Superman, Batman, The Flash, Archie, Donald Duck, and many more. In the process of selecting a couple of comic books for 10 cents each, one could peruse several others before making this important decision. As I grew, my love for the comics gradually faded away and magazines became more

Compelling Journey

important. Those early years created a reading pattern that would last the rest of my life. I can't remember when I have not had a book in progress.

Audie Murphy

Earl Stubbs

I recall Dr. Smith as being a reticent man and not prone to amusement. He died during the 40's prior to the building of the local hospital. His son Wendell was not a bundle of laughs either. He was a portly man prone to Stetson hats, string ties, and expensive cowboy boots. His jeans were always a bit too short and his dark hair was combed back in the style of the day. I always got the impression that Wendell was more content in the company of Big Boy, his grand champion Hereford bull, than at any other time.

Lois, on the other hand, was an outgoing person prone to laughter. While she was businesslike at work, things changed dramatically when her buddies from Marietta came in the store. Their conversations could be clearly heard in the next block and their laughter was rich and infectious.

Smith's Drug Store took on a different role during our middle school years. While it was the source for wonderful tasting treats and the latest comic books. It gradually became a place to spend time with girls after school. I am not sure if other Naples school kids took advantage of Smith's for that purpose, but our group did. We spent our free time at school playing sports and didn't spend time with girls. However, after school, we all headed to Smith's, grabbed the back tables, and nursed Cokes for the better part of an hour. This was

Compelling Journey

where we discussed who liked who and made plans for the next spin-the-bottle party. It was hard to say which part of the Smith's Drugstore lifestyle I would miss the most when it all came to and end.

I had always viewed both Wendell and Lois as a positive part of my life when growing up in Naples. Not many days passed without visiting the drugstore or speaking to them on the streets so it came as no surprise when either Billy Brunette or Richard Cole, who both worked at the drugstore, approached me about working there. I was in the eight grade and beginning to think about the world of work even though making such a major change in my lifestyle was no easy decision even at the ripe old age of 14.

I rather liked my life the way it was. I was especially enamored with Saturdays and Sundays. I had radio programs to listen to on Saturday, shows to watch, games to play, hamburgers to eat, and the general excitement of a weekend in Naples to consider. I postulated that if I went to work, I would necessarily have to give up most of those activities. The upside, of course, would be that I would have more money at my disposal. However, the money argument was not a strong one. Smith's paid 35 cents per hour which was the going rate for young hired help. The money would not change my life in any major way. Unlike several of the other guys in my crowd, I had more than one source for spending money. The major source was my Aunt Ella who provided the bulk of my meager funds. If Aunt Ella was not disposed to cough up the 25 cents or 50 cents I needed, I approached her daughter Ellie and put the mooch on her. In addition, my Uncle Dud was always a soft touch when he was home. If push came to shove, I could appropriate a few coins from my dad who lived next door. So money was not a problem considering my limited needs.

However, some of my buddies were going to work. I had always considered Smith's Drugstore as my favorite hang out in the entire town. I liked the owners and knew Richard Cole and Billy Brunette who had worked there for years. I decided to give it a shot.

The work was routine. I served drinks, sold books, and kept the elaborate fountain running. There was work after school and on weekends. Saturdays were long and busy. Three employees were kept busy behind the counter from Saturday morning to after midnight with short breaks for lunch and dinner. Late Saturday night was devoted to cleaning the fountain from top to bottom and preparing various mixes for the next week. The only job I didn't know how to accomplish was the mixing of chocolate syrup. The senior soda jerk, Richard Cole,

Compelling Journey

always mixed that mysterious concoction. It only consisted of milk and chocolate syrup out of a gallon can, but the proportions were of grave importance. He was, after all, a high school senior practically on his way to college. I don't remember why Richard was not at work that Saturday night but for whatever the reason, the new batch of chocolate syrup for Sunday did not get mixed.

The next day was the last day of my short tenure at Smith's Drugstore. The Sunday afternoon movie was underway and business was non-existent. This period of inactivity was the most difficult for me because I really enjoyed the Sunday afternoon movies. The only people in the store were Wendell and me when a gentleman from out of town dropped in for a bit of refreshment. I had seen the man before and recall that he was in the insurance business. For some reason, Wendell chose to make an impression on this man. He commented that the milkshakes were the best in the state and asked would the gentleman like one. The man said that he would. I started to prepare the milkshake only to discover that there was no chocolate syrup. I told Wendell that we were out of chocolate syrup assuming that he would know the formula for the mix and quickly make up a batch.

Earl Stubbs

To this day, I don't know if he didn't hear me but after a bit, he came charging behind the counter in a rage and proceeded to prepare the milkshake himself. I noticed that he poured the chocolate syrup directly from the gallon can. What a novel idea, I thought to myself. Why didn't I think of that? Wendell said no more about the incident but I could tell that he was furious. Even so it was a surpise when work was over for the day that Lois called me aside and informed me that my service were no longer needed at Smith's Drugstore. I have always wondered why Lois and not Wendell broke the news.

After I was over the initial embarrassment of the termination, I analyzed the situation as best I could at my age and from my own perspective. I faced the fact that I must have not been a very good employee. I must have deserved what I got or my good friends Wendell and Lois would have been more patient during my training period. I came to the further realization that not all of my acquaintances were my friends. They were just business people making their way through life.

There were positives that came out of the severance. I realized that I could go to the Sunday afternoon movie rather than work. I could jump in the car and go places with my friends whenever I wished. I could read as much as I liked without being pressed for time. I could

Compelling Journey

play sandlot ball and hang out at Don Nance's snowcone stand during the lazy summer days.

There was a down side as well. I would never be comfortable again in my favorite place of business in Naples. I could never drop in after school for a Coke without discomfort. As a result, I avoided Smith's Drugstore for the next four years unless it was for a special occasion or to fulfill needs for magazines. The store stopped being a part of my life and became a place of business. I would still go in the store but would conduct my business and leave. In later years it was even a chore to collect the free milkshakes Wendell provided for touchdowns but I swallowed my pride for those.

My negative dealings with the Smiths did not end there. During the summer before my senior year, I was keeping the company of a young lady from Tulsa who visited for the summer. I don't remember whose idea it was, but when she went back home, I felt compelled to provide a parting gift. She was a smoker, so I gave her a nice butane lighter from Smith's. It cost $12 and I charged it. I could lay my hands on $2 but not $12.

I began my senior year and gave little thought to the $12 I owed. Don't ask me how it was supposed to get paid. I knew my Aunt didn't like the girl from Tulsa so I could not bear to break the bad news of the gift. Not a word was said about the $12 during the coming months until it was time for Lois Smith to send out the year end bills. Naturally, I got one. My Aunt Ella quickly paid the bill but that was another instance of embarrassment brought on by a dumb decision on my part.

The point of this story is that my bad experience with my first job lasted a lifetime. I had to learn the difference between friends and acquaintances. I had to learn that lack of communication can be damaging, that life is not always fair, and that not everyone loves me. Even though I proved myself in the work arena time and time again with success after success, there has always been the smidgen of doubt in the back of my mind that began on that Sunday afternoon. Was I ever good enough? Would I ever be?

That was not to be the last time I was fired. Toward the end of my career, I held a national position in an international firm and was caught up in downsizing. My corporate home for eighteen years punished me for being fifty-seven years old and having a significant salary. When my pathetically incompetent supervisor explained to me that I was not losing my job because of the quality of my work, I felt a sense of relief. I lost my job but felt relieved because it was not because of something stupid that I had done.

Compelling Journey

Why didn't Richard Cole mix that chocolate syrup like he was supposed to do? Maybe I would have become president ... or not.

Earl Stubbs

38

As always, victory finds a hundred fathers but defeat is an orphan—Count Ciano

The Bomb
1952

Age 17

The Bomb was a 1939 Chevrolet that represented the residue of the failed marriage between Ellie and John L.

Compelling Journey

Barker. In 1940, he departed for San Francisco and left her with the car and the payments. By 1953, the once-proud automobile was but a shadow of its former self, but it was my one and only mode of transportation. The top speed going downhill was seventy miles per hour. The maroon paint faded to different shades, and the fenders were without symmetry. The inside of the ancient relic had an old car smell.

Ellie was the principal driver until I procured my driver's license at the age of twelve. We parked the vehicle in an old barn. It had two swinging doors on each end. If one approached the doors carefully, there was room for the car to squeeze in with three or four inches to spare. Ellie's idea of parking in the barn was to estimate the opening, get a running start, and then shut her eyes. The result was that the car careened back and forth between sides until it crashed into the door at the other end. It was an effective way of parking, but the fenders suffered. Every four or five years, Ellie took the Bomb to the Chevrolet dealership and had the fenders straightened. That was the only time the car got a bath as well. After she parked the car a few times, the disfigured fenders returned.

Several students in my class had the use of nice cars. Of all the automobiles that provided transportation to the

Earl Stubbs

Pewitt School and on dates from our area, the Bomb was by far the most esthetically challenged. When I was behind the wheel of our family car, I was not a proud driver.

After graduation from Pewitt High School in 1953, I spent the summer lifting watermelons, swimming at Daingerfield State Park, and killing time until classes at ET started in the fall. One hot, dusty evening, I drove around in the Bomb, seeking anything to eradicate the oppressive boredom and decided to drive past the rural home of an off-again, on-again girlfriend. We had dated intermittently for the past couple of years, but at the time, we were off again. The bloom had left the rose of our relationship the previous summer, when a slinky blond from Tulsa spent the summer visiting her aunt, who lived in the area. Meanwhile, I visited with the slinky blond that turned out to be one of those lose-lose situations. After the blond slinked back home, the young woman from Omaha and I still dated, but it was never the same. She was currently seeing one of the older guys from Naples, who had spent his time after graduation from Naples High School, flunking out of various institutions of higher learning.

I usually drove the Bomb to the extent of her limited capabilities. Therefore, it was not surprising that I enjoyed the sandy roads south of Omaha by spinning

Compelling Journey

hither and yon on that particular night. I came upon a sharp left turn and gunned the old girl. That was when I exceeded my driving skills and misjudged the importance of physics. The inertia of the machine responded to the forces of gravity, slid off the road, and flipped on her side.

The Bomb

After the car settled, the situation evolved into a period of silence broken only by the sound of the idling motor. I sat on the ground, or as much so as the passenger-side window would allow. Then, I glanced upwards and viewed the portion of the galaxy discernible through the opposite window. Gradually, it occurred to me that action on my part was necessary. I turned off the motor, climbed out of the open portal, and appraised the state of affairs. Learning nothing from my assessment, I attempted to push the car back over and failed. I had no choice but to swallow my pride, trudge back to Omaha, and beg for help from those rich farm boys who were always hanging around. As I started my embarrassing journey, I put aside my usual indifference to religion and prayed that the young woman and her new beau would not be out that night. My prayers went unanswered.

After a mile or so, I heard a car approaching from the rear. Fearing the worst, I made no effort to flag it down. There I was, walking down a deserted country road on a pitch-black night, and the car did not even slow down. A glance through the swirling dust confirmed that the car belonged to the young women's new beau. I was not surprised at his behavior. We had a history, and it was not a good one. My mortification knew no bounds.

Finally, a distant streetlight broke the gloom. I strode out of the darkness toward some of my Pewitt schoolmates, explained my predicament, and begged for assistance. They gave it freely since it gave them more time to ridicule. We soon arrived back at the scene, turned the car over, and I spun away in a cloud of righteous indignation.

When I arrived home, I parked the car in the barn and waited for a new day. After my work at the watermelon shed the next day, I went home to find Ellie

Compelling Journey

and Mama returning from a shopping trip to Mt. Pleasant. Taking the offensive, I suggested that the right side of the car sported fresh blemishes. Not being overly observant of such things, the women agreed that someone must have hit them while they were shopping. I agreed with their assessment, and the matter ceased to exist, except in my memory.

The Dirty Bomb

Earl Stubbs

39

God is always on the side of the big battalions—Voltaire

THE RUN

Age 18

Texas is famous for oil wells, rodeos, wide open spaces, and high school football among other things. The latter, a game of deception, dominance, and dexterity

Compelling Journey

first captured the hearts and minds of Texans around the turn of the century. I knew little of the sport until after World War II when we local yokels were introduced to sports magazines. I read articles about Johnny Lujak of Notre Dame, Choo Choo Justice of North Carolina, Smackover Scott of Arkansas, and our own homegrown version of the super football player, Doak Walker of SMU. In fact, the Doaker was the first college level player I ever saw perform. It was a game at the Cotton Bowl between SMU and Rice during FFA day at the state fair. The year was 1948.

Football is a diverse sport. Players with many dissimilar physical characteristics and skills are required to make up a team. The differences between an offensive tackle and a wide receiver are so vast that it makes one wonder if they play the same game. Quarterbacks, receivers, and runners are the skill players and must be able to manage the ball with consistency. Handling and throwing the ball is done primarily by the quarterback. Kicking is a key factor in the outcome of many games as well. For the linemen, football is a game of brute strength, manipulation, and creativity. The best players force their opponents to commit to courses that will result in failure. Football is far more kin to chess than most people realize.

Earl Stubbs

Speed, strength, and quickness are in constant use by all players. Quickness is used to put one in place to make a play, but unadorned speed may be the most precious commodity on a football field. Speed, when properly applied, cancels out all the other skills. Some football skills require years to develop and some players develop these skills to amazing levels. A defender may be smarter, stronger, and more talented but they still must catch the offensive player to apply any of these advantages and that is often impossible.

My senior year had not gone as well as I had hoped. After earning the starting running back position, I had several good games to my credit before the injury bug moved into my locker. At first there was a bursitis on my left heel, then a hip pointer that was excruciatingly painful for about ten days. Next came a severely sprained ankle. The latter caused me to miss most of the last couple of games. While I was rehabilitating with some efficiency, I was still not 100%.

I had hoped for a great season and a football scholarship to a small university but by the time the Daingerfield game was played, I realized that the scholarship was probably not going to happen. The coach was not my biggest fan at this time. He viewed my injuries as minor and my attitude that of a quitter. I was not to set foot on the field during the first half of the

Compelling Journey

Daingerfield game. My replacement got the carries and I got splinters.

Daingerfield had a good team. They had good size and speed but no great runner. Their quarterback, Richard Woods, was the most gifted athlete on the team. When he barked out the signals which were "ready, set," it sounded like "hada sue" so we called him "Hada Sue." A few members of our team responded to a special brand of humor.

We were doing better than expected so both teams were undefeated at the time the annual game rolled around. Daingerfield was expected to win but not by much. Their town was only 12 miles from our school so we knew most of their players and liked them for the most part. However, the rivalry was intense. Since their school was considerably larger than ours, we had not beaten Daingerfield since the war.

The first half produced a defensive standoff. It was three downs and kick, back and forth. Finally, Hada Sue found a receiver behind our safety and in an instant, the score was 7-0 in favor of Daingerfield. However, near the end of the first half, our diminutive fullback, Bobby Presley, caught what was perceived by the officials as a fumble on the dead run and scored. I clearly saw the play and the ball hit the ground and bounced into his arms. It was in reality little more than an incomplete forward pass and a loss of down for Daingerfield, but who were we to argue with the officials. We missed the extra point, so when the half ended, the score was Daingerfield 7 and Pewitt 6. The coach began to worry.

As we moved back toward the field while the band march, the assistant coach took me aside. He was my basketball coach and I was his captain, so we got on pretty good at the time. He explained that the football coach didn't think I wanted to play. He said that in order for me to play, I needed to tell the head coach I wanted to play. That struck me as being odd since I was all suited out to play football and had attended all the practices, but I went along with the game. I sought out the head coach and suggested that maybe he could put me in the game. He agreed to do so and immediately put me in the receiving position for the opening kickoff. After we lined up, I stood on about the 10-yard line of the South goal waiting for the whistle to begin the second half.

Every fan stood as the whistle finally sounded and the Daingerfield team advanced toward the ball. It was a huge kick, a high floater sailing with the north wind, but I could see it was coming to me. I took a few steps back, with my eyes fastened on the ball, and made the catch. The game was on.

Compelling Journey

The crowd noise reached a crest, but strangely enough, football players don't hear much crowd noise. They hear the slap of pads and the grunt of effort. While no game is faster than football, this play unreeled in slow motion, individual combat, and maximum effort on the part of the players.

The plan called for a run up the middle. After I took my first few steps in that direction, I could see no real avenue to the goal line. Like most running backs, I used my vision and instincts to best take advantage of the efforts of my teammates and the mistakes of my opponents. Almost immediately, a tackler detached himself from that mass of humanity and moved in my direction. Just as suddenly, a player with a uniform of blue and grey blind-sided him out of the picture. So far, so good but I still had about 80 yards to go.

Immediately, a second tackler challenged me on the 30-yard line. He looked a bit heavy, so I slammed my left foot into the turf and leaned right. He instantly responded and moved to his left. That was a mistake. I planted my right foot and slid opposite of his motion. All he could do was reach out with a powerful arm and try to knock me off balance. He almost succeeded, but I managed to spin completely around and left him clutching air. 60 yards to go.

Earl Stubbs

The defensive scheme for covering a kickoff is like a funnel. Tacklers usually cover the breadth of the field and gradually move inward toward the ball. Battles went on all around me. Tacklers were striving to annihilate me, and my blockers were just as determined to protect the ball.

Only seconds had passed since the whistle, but it seemed an eternity. The third and last tackler I faced was the safety. He waited at the 50-yard line. I knew this kid. He was smart and very fast. I would not be able to juke him, and I would need to get past him if I was to score. To accomplish such a feat seemed unrealistic at the time and conditions looked bleak.

Running backs have this instinct thing. The good ones are able to see any player within their vision, but they do not focus on any one player. They see the field as a game board. I sensed a friend coming up on the outside. A glance told me that it was my best buddy, Donald Dawson, who was a tall lanky end. He was a deadly blocker. I ran ahead of him, and the rest of the players were coming up fast. I had little choice but to slam on the brakes and allow him to take a shot at the safety.

He knifed past me and hurled his 6' 4" frame at the opposing tacker. Just when the safety thought all of him was past, the legs came along and turned him a complete

Compelling Journey

flip. I planted my right foot, charged hard left, and ran for daylight.

The opportunity was there. I could not see behind me, but that was not a concern. Nobody would catch me from behind. For some reason the crowd noise begin to break through my consciousness. Something very special was happening, and I had long since shifted into overdrive. It was then just a matter of doing what I did best and that was pick my feet up and put them down faster than anyone else on the field.

Even though the entire run had taken less than 15 seconds, it appeared to last a month. Finally, I covered the last few of the 95 yards and drifted into the end zone. The ref raised his hands signifying a touchdown. In those days there was no spiking of the ball or celebrations of any kind. The prevailing philosophy was to act like you had been in the end zone before, and that it was no big deal. I handed the ball to the ref, turned, and observed the roaring crowd. I saw my teammates running full tilt toward me. I watched the dejection on the faces of the Daingerfield players. It was to last the remainder of the game. The picture would last me a lifetime.

During the late 80's Pewitt High School reached the state quarter finals, and I decided to go to the game.

Earl Stubbs

During the halftime, I met a former player who graduated several years after me. He was a retired Dallas police officer and an interesting man. He said to me as we were starting back up into the stands to watch the second half, "I saw the run." "What run?" I asked. "The run against Daingerfield," he replied and then he went on to describe the run almost yard by yard as seen through the eyes of a young boy who loved the game of football. He brought it all back. So even though the run amounted to nothing in the annals of Pewitt football lore, it meant something to that young boy and it meant something to me.

It is interesting that in spite of my myriad of injuries, Catfish Smith, the head coach at East Texas State saw something in the skinny kid from Pewitt who could punt, pass, and run. He offered me a full ride. The injury bug influenced me more than him, so I declined.

Compelling Journey

40

**To win without risk is a triumph without glory—
Pierre Corniell**

THE QUAGMIRE
1952

One of the driest summers on record in East Texas resulted in a severe drought in 1952. You can imagine our surprise when we got off the bus in Clarksville for the 1952 district championship game and saw that the field was a virtual quagmire of mud. Such conditions subtracted greatly from our team. We relied on speed and quickness.

We were still very confident. I recall that both Clarksville and DeKalb had already defeated Atlanta, so a victory in Clarksville would seal the championship for our school. Even when we started wading through the mud during our warm-ups, which was strange since it had not rained in East Texas in months, we felt good about the outcome.

Earl Stubbs

The Clarksville game was important for us, and we were highly motivated. They had already suffered one defeat at the hands of a good DeKalb team and we were undefeated. However, for all of our formations our team usually won with defense. Ramey was an excellent defensive coach, but his first love was offense. To give the edge to his team in this important game, Coach Ramey chose to put in a completely new offensive scheme.

As one of our running backs, I had some speed, could throw a little, and kick a little. Ramey believed that if a coach had a gun, he should shoot it. During the four days before the Clarksville game, Ramey taught and coached the spread formation or what is now called the modern day "shotgun." I became the new tailback and when using the spread, passed, ran, or kicked the ball on every offesnive play. Of course even the practices tended to wear me down, so by Friday, I was about pooped.

In addition to the new formation, Ramey developed a cagey misdirection play to begin the game. It worked great in practice against the second team. It was designed to break the back of Clarksville on the first play of the game with Don Dawson's crack-back block.

We started out in the split T formation in the first series, but for some strange reason, the exchange

Compelling Journey

between Billy Williams and the all-district center, Jack Harvey, didn't work. No problem, we would just try again. Same result. The exchange didn't work. Finally, the Clarksville team figured out what we were trying to do, and they nailed us for a loss. However, a nice 70 yard punt by our newly anointed hero pinned them back and our defense forced a punt. On the next series, Coach Ramey called for the spread formation and I lined up in the tailback slot.

When one runs the ball from the spread formation, the center must deliver the ball to a moving target about seven yards deep ... sometimes left, sometimes right. I moved to my left on that play, as we practiced all week, but in the excitement of the moment, the ball went straight back. I attempted to recover the ball, and as I bent down to pick it up, both Clarksville ends buried me, and in the process, tore ligaments in my ankle. I was finished.

I thought Coach Ramey would scrap the spread and revert back to the split T. I assumed incorrectly. Billy Williams had practiced the new formation from another position, but he was a good football player. He proceeded to step into the role of tailback with virtually no practice in the position. He hurled his 150-pound body at the big Clarksville team time and time again. I marveled when he got up after absorbing the punishment he took. He just kept running, throwing, and kicking the ball for the rest of the night. I witnessed every ball game Billy Williams ever played and in my mind, that was his finest hour. He was likely the only member of the Pewitt team who could really be proud of his accomplishments that night. Unfortunately, Billy's heroics could not salvage the game, and the Pewitt Brahmas went down to defeat.

The next day, I had an ankle the size of a grapefruit, and to compound matters, my sister Dorothy had a wedding planned. I rode with Mr. and Mrs. Bean, the Superintendent of Schools, and we attended the wedding in Chandler, Texas.

PEWITT HIGH SCHOOL

Compelling Journey

41

The point of living and of being an optimist, is to be foolish enough to believe the best is yet to come--Peter Ustinov

THE PEWITT HIGH SCHOOL CLASS OF 1953

There was nothing commonplace about the members of the Paul H. Pewitt High School class of 1953. We were a special group, at least in our own eyes, and reunions are not held so much in commemoration of graduation but more as a celebration of the journey that preceded that day. A few of us spent the better part of twelve years sharing our lives on a daily basis. Such relationships are not easily forgotten nor should they be. They become ever more precious as the years pass. A few of us started school together in the fall of 1941 and remained together for the entire journey. This is our story.

Earl Stubbs

When we gathered together for the first time in September of 1941, our primary emotion was excitement and our primary concern was about who was going to care for us. Who would replace our parents or guardians as the source of our comfort? In our case, her name was Gladys Martin and she was near the end of a long and illustrious teaching career. Under the tutelage of Mrs. Martin, we came to learn that there was more to school than recess and that our personal comfort was no longer the center of the universe.

Mrs. Gladys Martin taught first grade at the grade school in Naples in 1941 and there was only one such class. She was a slight, dark haired lady who had already taught most of the parents and relatives of the members of our new class. Her house was located next door to the school. It would be an understatement to say that her sense of humor was limited. However, she was scrupulously fair, and we prospered under her care.

Mrs. Martin guided us through that hellish year that saw the Japanese attack Pearl Harbor, that saw the world engulfed in war, and that saw us snatched from the security of our homes and hurled into the cauldron of social interaction that would mold our very being. Our world consisted of bells, homework, brushing teeth, pungent restrooms, fickle water fountains, reciting, ciphering, reading, cutting and pasteing, curbing our

Compelling Journey

childish ways, and as the days grew cool, matters of warmth. During the winter months, we listened to the hiss of the ancient steam heating system that seemed to keep the temperature either freezing cold or near equatorial heat as the condensation ran down the windows and made strange patterns.

Much was happening in our world other than warfare. In 1941 Glen Miller's Chattanooga Choo Choo topped the charts, Arsenic and Old Lace was the hit of Broadway, Citizen Kane won the Oscar, and The Maltese Falcon with Humphrey Bogart was a big hit as well. Penicillin came into use, F. Scott Fitzgerald penned The Last Tycoon, Joe Dimaggio hit in 56 straight games, Whirlaway won the triple crown, and the class of 1953 began school. This was no ordinary year.

Before we graduated, the allied powers introduced the atomic bomb to modern warfare, overran the forces of evil, and the greatest war came to an end. Many Naples residents came home from the services and began their postwar lives in our midst. The cold war between the Soviet Union and the USA began and proliferated. The "Police Action" in Korea began and ended in stalemate and frustration.

The city fathers funded a hospital in Naples and several doctors came to practice. I recall the Naples student days of one such physician. He was James Leeves, M. D., and he graduated from Naples High School.

Twelve years of academics, literature, theater, movies, and social interactions made impressions on our psyche. Some presentations were Porgy and Bess, Bambi, Casablanca, Oklahoma, My Friend Flicka, National Velvet, and Mrs. Minerva just to name a few. As we moved through the grades following the war, football suits, basketball uniforms, and band uniforms were dusted off and put back into use. Near the end of our run, we received a taste of the future world as we watched snowy figures on television for the first time and the power of radio was forever altered. While only a few members of the class had telephones, any suggestion of something as extraordinary as the Internet would not have registered in our wildest dreams.

The quality of our school building was deplorable. The newer school, which was an ancient relic itself, was the high school. The grade school was the really old one. The building had been condemned for years but in a rural Texas town, where the depression was still a fact of life, there was just no money for anything better. We didn't know that our school was a wreck. We didn't know that we had few books and little in the way of school supplies. We had pencils, crayons, a Big Chief

Compelling Journey

tablet, an imaginative teacher, and the will to learn. For some of us, the time spent at school was the best part of our lives. I was one of those.

Like most students making their way through school, we clicked with some teachers and didn't click with others. I was never a teacher's favorite, but I managed peaceful coexistence with most. The only teacher whoever used any sort of violence on my person was a grade school teacher named Louise Davis. She was never my teacher, but I was frightened to death of the woman. I was always on my best behavior when she was around. One day I walked up the stairs to my fifth grade room not daring to even make a peep. When I drew abreast of her at the top of the stairs, she smacked me hard in the face. She didn't tell me why and I never asked.

I must say that Exa Tolbert in fourth grade and Pete Adams in the eighth grade were my favorites in grade school. Leonard Prewitt, the high school principal, was my favorite in high school. He taught chemistry. Mr. O. E. Miller, the agriculture teacher, was also a favorite. Who could forget Miller chasing students Jack Coker and Richard Cole through the streets of Naples as they all fired BB guns at each other. That is an unlikely scenario at the turn of the millenium. Most of my classmates in

Earl Stubbs

1941 made an indelible imprint on my memory. The boys in our class were especially fortunate. The reason being that not only did we have good teachers to show us the way, but we had a crop of really super girls to keep us in line as well. These girls set very high standards for us boys and those gifts carried over into our adult lives. They were terrific young ladies and grew into exceptional women. Even though some are mothers and even grandmothers by this time, I would be most uncomfortable watching an R rated movie in their presence.

The boys were just as great. They were intelligent, athletic, and talented. Most went on to successful careers which must have surprised many of our teachers. We were not the most disciplined group ever to come along, so we left a string of frustrated but impressed teachers as we moved along.

Several boys made the entire journey from first grade to graduation. Jack Harvey joined the class a few weeks after school began in 1941 and became the All American Boy in more ways than one. Jack was tall, handsome, and very bright. He was a dominant football player and a good all around athlete. He was always ready to answer any challenge that came along. He retired after a long and successful career as a teacher and principal in public education.

Compelling Journey

Tommy Walls started and finished with the class. Tommy was an exceptional scholar, musician, and was a member of the all state band. For personal reasons, Tommy chose not to attend class reunions.

A. J. was considered by his teachers and most members of the community to have limited intellectual ability. Poor grades prevented him from profiting from his significant ability as a football player.

Bobby Presley, known as, pound for pound, the toughest kid in the class, lived on a working farm. He woke up early to milk the cows before school, and he had chores after school as well. Bobby was a fierce football player at 150 pounds and played fullback and linebacker. He is one of the best people I know. We spent many wonderful days riding our bikes over country roads and enjoying the fruits of nature.

Coy Moreland got off to a slow start. He was not the best reader or the fastest runner but when the race was over, he broke the tape first. I remember Coy blossoming academically in the ninth grade though it probably happened before that. Coach Bill Bishop was our very creative history teacher, and he developed a teaching system that allowed him to teach without being present. He designed the class so that each student developed as many questions as possible over the current chapter.

Earl Stubbs

The student who created the most questions ask his/her questions to the other class members. Coy was always the one who asked the questions.

It is amazing how hard we worked and how much we learned under Coach Bishop's system. Coy also spoke algebra which was a foreign tongue to many of us. Don't ask me where he learned to type, but Coy was a whiz at that as well and always represented the school in typing contests. He became the most gifted academic male member of the class and took these skills onto Texas A & M and a successful career.

Randall Raines went the distance. He was another of those smiling people. Randall was very good natured and his family was active in providing summer jobs for many of our classmates. Randall had a horse as well and if my memory serves, it was a paint. I recall that it was a very pretty horse, and Randall rode in all the parades.

One classmate in first grade made an intense impression that lasted for decades. She was a perky young lady fashioned after the movie starlet Shirley Temple. During the early years, grades were everything and she was just about perfect. She never missed an answer, and she delivered her answers with great charm even though her smile lacked a few teeth. One of the most impressive aspects of this student was her footwear. She had the most delightful boots that had a

Compelling Journey

small pocket for a knife. I was green with envy. But alas, after only a year in our midst, she moved away and I never saw her again. Her name was Shirley McCoy.

My recollections of the student who would arguably become the best athlete of our class was one of concern. I remember him on the first day of school in a yellow one piece cotton garment called a playsuit. He did not like his playsuit and he did not like the idea of his mother leaving him alone at school. It took a couple of days for things to settle down for this young man. As I recall the future quarterback of our football team, Billy Williams, didn't wear playsuits anymore.

Some class members established themselves as great characters for their names if for no other reason. Two such students were Sunshine Franklin and Sambo Jones. Sunshine was a freckled, white haired child who struggled with academics but was ahead of the rest of us in many other ways. With the exception of A. J. Wells, he was the only class member to climb to the top of the city water tower. That was no small feat for a six-year-old. He taught us all how to steal ice cream and soft drinks by entering the school building after hours. He taught us how to torment girls, and he was always the first to hear the latest little moron joke. Sunshine never made it through school, and even when he joined the air force, he spent some of his time in military prison. He was, however, never malicious and whatever he did, a smile adorned his freckled face. He eventually became a plumber in Dallas, fathered several children, and eventually died in an automobile accident at a relatively young age. I just know that somewhere there is a white-haired youngster making his way up a water tower with a huge grin on his face.

Bobby Ray Brock was sort of an in and out member of our class. He was not attuned to academics, and as soon as he was old enough, he was pulled out of school each year to work in the Hampton sawmill to help feed his family. Bob was a dominant athlete and spent many years in the USAF as an athlete. He could do it all. He was eligible to play football and baseball our senior year, and we fielded a solid football team in 1952. Bob was a big contributor to the team that defeated Linden, New Boston, Hooks, Daingerfield, Hughes Springs, and DeKalb among others. However, Bob found his niche with the Texas Highway Department and became a high level administrator with that organization. He was another of our classmates who was self-made and successful.

We gained status through games and acts of leadership, and this class had plenty of leaders. During the early years, recess was built around two rather high

Compelling Journey

swings, monkey bars for climbing, a seesaw, and a two level bar for chinning. Daredevil A. J. Wells once swung so high that he went over the top and fell. Fortunately, he was not badly injured.

The girls pretty much went their own way and the boys went their way. The boys would find stones that resembled a handgun and run and shoot like the cowboys we saw each Saturday at the Inez Theater.

The members of the class of 1953 did not spend all of their time in school. Naples was such a wonderful place to grow up in the 1940's as was most small Texas towns. The social center of life in Naples was Saturday night. Not that many people had cars in those days and Saturday was when supplies for the entire week were purchased in the town stores and transported home. Semi-taxi services were common where a pickup truck served to transport groceries home for a fee or this same pickup might transport a cow to market for someone who had no vehicle.

Saturday usually started for me early in the morning when I listened to some of my favorite radio programs such as "Let's Pretend." Then at about 1:00 p.m., the Inez theater opened and we were treated to a cowboy movie for the outrageous price of $.09. If it was a good week, we might spend another $.05 for popcorn. The movie consisted of a comedy-Donald Duck was a favorite, a short subject-usually The Three Stooges, Movie Tone News-usually war news, and the feature movie staring Gene Autry, Roy Rogers, or any one of a large group of fast drawing cowboy heros who often took time out for a song. We never saw the movie just once. We stayed for the second showing, and this was not always easy since the theater did not have a restroom. Finally, we would leave the darkened theater and after our eyes became accustomed to the light, we would start up the street leaping up and touching signs, which was one of our several rites of passage. The first sign any of us could touch was Mrs. Tabb's variety store. The last one we could touch was Heard's dry goods. After a person could touch Heard's sign, the game was just about over.

After a hamburger or an evening meal to recharge our batteries, we headed back to town. The early evening was spent chasing each other around the alleyways, playing fox and hound, or shooting off fireworks. Of course, Sunshine Franklin was the one who put a cherry bomb in the city restroom and blow up the commode.

The town did not shut down easily on Saturday. The soda fountains finally closed well after midnight. The midnight show began about 11 p.m., and let out about 1 a.m. Most of us did not attend the midnight show until we were older. The Inez Theater showed a completely

Compelling Journey

different movie on Sunday, and it usually was the best of the week. Add in Sunday School and church on Sunday and a 1940's Naples weekend was quite an affair. It was better than all the TV and video games in the world.

Earl Stubbs

42

**Poets and philosophers are the unacknowledged legislators of the world—
Percy Bysshe Shelley**

OLD ET

Tejas Pledge class of 1953

Compelling Journey

To prove that a storehouse of memories is prone to idealization, I recall the summer of 1953 as being one of vivid colors, lazy cumulous clouds backed by a cerulean sky, and a total absence of discomfort. Thunderstorms, searing heat, and boredom absented themselves from this idyllic summer unless it was the smell of wet sand after the sun burst through. I call to mind slicing through the tepid water of Daingerfield State Park after diving from the high board. Underneath the platform, with the aid of a mask, I recall going nose to nose with small black bass enjoying the shade and crystal water of the lake. I recall picking up literally thousands of sixty-pound watermelons during the season in Naples as my Florida born stacker loaded boxcar after boxcar with the black diamonds for shipping around the nation.

I gave little thought to the upcoming school year when my life would change so dramatically. My senior year at Paul Pewitt School merged into a history, and a new adventure at East Texas State Teachers College lurked on the horizon.

My cousin and benefactor, Ellie Barker, along with a Pewitt classmate's mother, Rita Nance, journeyed to Commerce, found us a room, and scouted out the institution. Don Nance, my future roommate, and I went about our summer business and awaited the upcoming

Earl Stubbs

day when we would actually changed our addresses, take care of our own business, and make our own decisions. The latter freedom proved to be to our detriment.

The thought of attending East Texas State Teachers College in Commerce, Texas, held no terror for me. I was the third of my immediate family to attend the college. Since we were not a bookish family, none in the Stubbs family had a college degree before us and few owned a high school diploma. My sister, Marvalynn Stubbs, convinced herself that a college education made a difference. She was the first member of the family to graduate from college, and our sister, Dorothy Jean Stubbs followed in her footsteps.

Dot, as she was known, showed her annuals to me during infrequent visits, and built her fellow students into campus deities in my eyes. Additionally, I visited the campus during my high school days usually pertaining to an athletic event. Both of my coaches were ET alumni as were most of my teachers. The campus was about 70 miles from my hometown of Naples. It was just far enough to prevent too many trips home but not so far that we could not hitch hike there if necessary.

We had little conception of the impact fellow Naples students would have on our entire time at the college. Several of the more troublesome ones, such as Jack Coker and Richard Cole, just took up where they left off

Compelling Journey

at Naples High School albeit with a more mature demeanor. They helped us make decisions that were not always in our best interests such as spending far more time pledging a social club than frequenting the library. As much as I would like to blame them for my shortcomings, the literal fault nestles in my own bosom.

We had no more than unloaded our meager possessions in our room for two at the corner of Hunt and West Neal Streets than our friends from Naples came out of the woodwork. They offered opinions on which professors to choose, when to schedule our classes, which classes to take, and the time and place for the Tejas Social Club smoker.

My personal goals differed from past behavior. I wanted to avoid any ties with a contrived social life and devote myself to study for the first time in my life. Since declining a football scholarship due to my diminutive size and propensity for injury, I felt an obligation to my foster sister, who worked as a nurse, to see me through to graduation. I did not take into account my personality.

There were reasons why I had never devoted myself to scholarship. I was ADD but didn't know it. I was enamored with young females and did know it. So my natural social, extrovert driven needs quickly booted academia and dedication right out the window. I fell into the social scene, pledged the Tejas Club, and achieved membership during the first semester.

Don Nance and I started in first grade together. The only problem with my living conditions was that the other roommate was a former Paris Junior College lineman who liked to wrestle. Don was a tackle on our football team, and he liked to wrestle as well. They both like to wrestle with me. Every time the furniture started to fly, the property owner would stick her head in the phone nook and scold us. I was always grateful though I never lost to either one.

Don didn't like the interference, so he arranged for us to move at the end of the semester. We hooked up with Don Dawson from Naples, a transfer from Kilgore Junior College, and moved into an apartment house. Dawson was my best friend since first grade and had left KJC when he lost his basketball scholarship. Across the hall were two guys from Farmersville and one from Wolfe City. As the decades passed, they had a much more influence on my life than the Naples boys. Stanley Stooksberry evolved into a life-long friend. Bill Jacobs became my brother-in-law. They both died early. Dale Gaskell, the most stable of the bunch, earned his doctorate and did everything right for the rest of his life.

After about six weeks, Don Nance joined the Air Force, and Don Dawson dropped out to become an

Compelling Journey

electrician. That left me without roommates. I moved in with Stan Stooksberry, Bill Jacobs, and Dale Gaskill.

After a couple of visits to Friendly Farmersville, The hometown of Stan and Bill, I met and began dating Bill's sister, Nancy. 58 years later, we are still dating. In fact, we have a date tonight to watch a rented movie from our twin recliners.

The next three years of my time at ET were topsy turvy. There were good times and bad. The details are personal. I will share that I was elected president of the Tejas Club and have since earned the Golf Blazer award for alumni activities. I am something of a celebrity at the university, and received several honors along the way. The bottom line is that I had enough grade points to graduate in 1957.

A few years later, I earned my masters from North Texas State University, where I was a devoted and successful scholar. Go figure!

43

Any plan conceived in moderation must fail when the circumstances are set in extremes—Prince Clemons Von Metternich

THE PANTY RAID

Alice Kaiser, third girl from left, second row, unlocked the back door of Binnion Hall.

During the ETSTC school year of 1955-56, several East coast universities staged and executed campus events known as panty raids. In order to protect the reputations of the students, universities severely segregated male and female students with regards to domiciles. There were girl's dorms and boys dorms and never the twain should meet. These daring young men gained entrance to the female dorms and ran helter, skelter through the buildings in search of ladies undergarments. In many cases, they were successful in their quest. These episodes made national news, horrified the country, and prompted two inhabitants of the Tejas Social Club House to create an evening of fun that had stood the test of time 49 years later. Here's what happened.

After wearing out my academic welcome at ET, I retreated to the peace and quiet of the Kilgore Junior College campus for the spring semester. I quickly forged a reputation as a studious person and gained the respect of student and faculty alike.

One of my schoolmates was a navy vet named Bud Smith. Ironically, he had shared time in the shore patrol with a former Artema named Joe Terrell who was my brother-in-law at the time. At 5' 5", Bud must have struck terror into the hearts of wayward sailors while performing his duty.

After an uneventful spring at KJC, I went back for another shot at ET in the fall. As it turned out, Bud followed me. I liked Bud, and it was only natural that I would invite him to join the Tejas Club of which I was already a member. Bud joined and pledged. We ended up being roommates at the Tejas House near the campus.

I had never lived in such a public place before and it was not always easy to get to sleep especially in light of the fact that a group of rowdy Delta County boys were in the next room. At any rate, Bud and I were attempting to talk ourselves to sleep one fateful night during late winter or early spring. Our thoughts and conversation moved to a discussion of those students in the Northeast who staged the panty raids. To be brutally honest, we were both a bit jealous of their notoriety.

It is impossible to remember who made the statement "We could do that." However, history proves that one of us did. At first, we were not completely serious. Then we started discussing logistics and got serious in a hurry. We decided that we would contact the leadership of the other men's social clubs and get their take on the idea. They were a bit more conservative than the Tejas, and most Tejas were a bit more conservative than Bud and me, so it was likely that they would turn up their collective noses at the plan, and we would get on with our lives.

I spoke with Richard Stevenson, the Artema President. To my great surprise, he thought it was a grand idea and agreed to have reps at the planned meeting behind the stadium in two days time. The Cavaliers, Friars, Ogimas, and Paragons jumped on the bandwagon as well, and a nice sized crowd gathered behind the stadium to discuss the matter.

Surrounded by men's social club members, my roommate, Bud Smith, got up in the bed of a pickup and laid out the big night. The plan was simplicity itself. Mrs. Gant, the housemother and queen of population control, closed down Binnion Hall and locked the doors at 10:30 p.m. However, a close and personal friend of mine, a Kalir with a winsome spirit, agreed to unlock the Northwest door at 11 p.m. After that, the troops could enter the building and pillage at will. Raincoats and a woman's stocking over our heads made up the dress code. We all swore, on pain of expulsion, that if caught, we would deny any knowledge or participation. Yeah right!

The night arrived. We gathered in several groups behind Binnion Hall and waited for zero hour. At the stroke of 11:00, someone, it could have been me, tried the door. To my great surprise, the door was actually unlocked and fellow clubbers started pouring through the door spreading out and gaining every floor. Of course, the girls all knew we were coming

Compelling Journey

At this point, it became personal. For the next ten minutes, every participant gained memories that will last a lifetime. Mine included charging up to the second floor and looking for a friendly face. I found one, took the offered panties, and headed for the exit. However, I glanced down the hall and saw Clyde "Red" Carroll, complete with stocking over his face, walking along chatting with the dorm mother, Mrs. Gant. Neither appeared to be overly excited.

The male students filled and cleared the dorm in short order with our mission accomplished. We all retired to various venues for celebration and recounted our experiences. We had our fun, and now the only remaining obstacle was to stay in school. That proved to be somewhat difficult.

Dean of Men, Dough Rollins, went to work early the next day. He began to call in social club members and offer them a deal. Give him names and stay in school. It didn't take long before a Paragon spilled his guts, and the Dean invited us in for a chat. When my turn came, I looked into his kindly face and asked, "What panty raid?" He countered with a letter to my father stating that there had been a panty raid and even though I had feigned innocence, Dean Rollins still considered me a prime suspect. The man was no dummy. Nothing more was done or said about the matter on an official basis.

It was a great night. All the social clubs worked in harmony, and we did no real harm except to the egos of the administration. Kent Biffle, award-winning columnist for the Dallas Morning News, was a student at that time. He wrote an article for the paper about the event many years later. It is still a topic of conversation when Tejas gather.

I attended the University homecoming fifty-three years later, and took a tour of the campus. A young faculty member was the guide. When we passed Binnion Hall, he referenced the Panty Raid. I looked out the window at the old building but said not a word.

Bud Smith passed at an early age but will remain a legend in the hearts and minds of us all for his part in the Great Binnion Hall Panty Raid.

Binnion Hall

44

It is the fashion to style the present moment an extraordinary crisis—Benjamin Disraeli

SALAD NIGHTS
1957

One early spring afternoon in 1957, I lounged at the Student Union Building with a couple of campus leaders. Two of us were presidents of ET social clubs. The other was the newly elected president of the ET student body, so as a group, we packed some campus political weight. This detail made the events of the next two days even more bizarre.

The student body president was in a more celebratory mode, so it was probably he who said the magic word beer. We considered the idea for at least thirty seconds before voting unanimously to make the trip to Red Coleman's on the outskirts of Big D. In those days, there was no running down to the local beer store and grabbing a six-pack or three. There were two places to obtain beer from Commerce in those days. One was Oklahoma. The other was Dallas. The Dallas trip was a tad longer but more scenic. Nobody bought six-packs. Everyone bought cases. After all, the going rate was $2.50.

Obtaining permission from Nancy was not a problem. Our firstborn was incubating, and she likely could do without making dinner. It didn't hurt that one of the three was her brother and my brother-in-law. We jumped into my black/white 1950 Ford Fairlane with custom interior and hit the road. The fact that my car was well known on campus was another factor that did not register during our decision making process.

Driving and drinking was the order of the day. Only the unlucky or stupid attracted enough attention on the way back from Dallas to get into trouble. We had almost made it out of Red Coleman's parking lot before we popped three cans.

We sipped our way back to Commerce and began to cruise the area and visit friends. Our condition did not endear us to many of them. At about 1 a.m., we cruised the downtown area for the 642nd time and noticed a fellow student, Artis Barnes, delivering produce to the grocery stores. The student body president thought it would be just delightful to grab a case or two of produce. We queried, "What on earth will we do with produce?"

One of the reasons for the election of our friend was that he was, by nature, very persuasive. Within a minute or two, he sold us on the idea, and we furtively avoided Artis who was working his way through college delivering food during the wee hours of the morning. SBP grabbed a case of cabbage and one of lettuce. Then we joyously fled the scene and drove to the Paragon clubhouse. Of course, everyone was asleep.

Refusing to abandon the moment, the student body president dumped both cases of produce into the bed of a sleeping club brother. Again, he did not use the best of judgment. The victim happened to be, James Ed Alexander, a former fleet light heavyweight champion while in the USN. Fortunately, after James Ed gathered his wits and saw the perpetrators, a grin appeared on his face. After all, we were both from Naples, and I had known him for most of my life.

After that final escapade, we had just about milked the event for all that it was worth. We drifted home and grabbed whatever sleep was left before first class. Or was it the second class?

The next day began uneventfully. I went to school, had lunch, and drove downtown for a haircut. My barber cut the best flattop found anywhere. When he finished, I strolled out to my fine black/white Ford only to find the local law-enforcement officer waiting with a smile on his face. He asked me if I owned the car. I admitted such. Then he went on to explain that a robbery had occurred the previous evening, and a witness saw my car in the area. He suggested that I collect my friends and meet with him and the produce company owner at the police station. *Uh oh*, I thought.

True to my word, I located my fellow gang members, and we spent what little time we had left attempting to figure out a way to beat this rap. Let's face facts. Two social club presidents and a Student Body President did not need this kind of heat. About all we could come up with was that we would play it by ear. What we didn't know was whether the rat had actually seen us taking the produce.

When we arrived, the police officer and the Big Cheese owner of the produce company waited. The officer explained that the monetary value of the stolen goods was $15. The BC just wanted his money back.

I saw an opportunity. I needed to know if we were actually seen making the heist, and I didn't believe that we were. I explained to the two men that I had parked my car at a social clubhouse for much of the night in question. Normally, in such a crime-free city, we left the keys in the car. It was not unusual for one of our friends to borrow the car to run errands or even go on a date, since we had so few cars available. We could not account for the whereabouts of the car for much of the night. By this time, the BC was nodding his head.

Earl Stubbs

I looked the man in the eyes and said, "Sir, we apologize for any inconvenience you may have suffered. We will cover any losses you incurred at this time. Rather than drag this thing out, we three will assume the guilt for our club brothers. We will also collect the money from the responsible parties, so we will be out nothing. If we must spend time in jail, then so be it. My only request is that I serve my time on weekends, since I graduate this semester, and I don't need to miss any classes."

By this time, the big cheese was nodding vigorously, and a solitary tear ran down his face. "Son," he said a quiver in his voice. "If you need any money before you get out of school, you just let me know."

Grinning from ear to ear, the police officer informed us that there would be no jail time or any other punishment under the circumstances. He suggested that we must be fine young men to be willing to shoulder the blame for our friends.

We shelled out the $15, shook hands all around, and headed back to the clubhouse where a few cans of ice-cold beer remained. Schlitz, I believe.

45

**Be always sure you are right---then go ahead—
David Crockett**

A MATTER OF HONOR

Before they left this vale of tears, my immediate family members called me Buddy. The only other living person to do so is James S. Leeves, M.D. I find the sound of my old nickname comforting when coming from him. Jimmy and I go back a few years.

My first recollection of him was in the summer of 1942. He attended Texas University at the time, and I had just finished the first grade. His brother Jerry still attended Naples School, and their parents operated a local pharmacy. I recall the smile of Mrs. Leeves, when one entered the store, and the dark pine floor cleaned daily with a mysterious tan powder. Jimmy was a quiet, pleasant young man who owned a whimsical smile. To say he was thin would be akin to saying Mt. Everest was tall.

Jimmy came and went for the next few years, as he graduated from college and medical school. Meanwhile, back at the home front, the local banker's son lost his life in World War II. His father donated the insurance from the fatality toward the construction of a hospital in Naples. The project came to fruition and two young physicians joined the staff. One was Dr. Charles Wise. The other was Dr. James Leeves. Another decade would pass before the latter's patients stopped calling him Jimmy and started calling him Dr. Leeves. He was still thin and still looked like a teenager.

My connection with the hospital was personal. My cousin/foster-sister, Ella Mae Barker, or "Ellie" as she was known in the family, became a nurse at the Naples Hospital and spent the bulk of her working life there.

When Ellie completed a shift, she would summarize the entire eight hours using the, I said, he/she said, method. At least, the summaries were more interesting than when she worked at a local café. As a result, the family remained well versed on personnel, patients, and events at the hospital. At home, she always referred to Dr. Leeves as Jimmy and his associate as Dr. Wise. When she had a serious problem, she always took it to Jimmy, but she called him Dr. Leeves.

1950 was not to be my year. In the summer, I swam across Glass Club Lake, a rite of passage, and experienced some abdominal discomfort. As the pain increased, I went to avail myself of the medical expertise of Dr. Leeves. He checked it out and gave me some antibiotics. I could tell he was not happy about the situation.

After a few more days, it became clear something was seriously amiss. Dr. Leeves pointed out that my stomach was "distended", which means that it was getting bigger. I was reasonably sure I was not pregnant. He scheduled surgery. Dr. Wise would do the honors with Dr. Leeves attending.

They chose a spinal block for anesthesia, because Dr. Leeves discovered that when he set a bone in my arm, the general anesthetics of the day were not for me. While I was not in excessive pain during the procedure, I swear I felt every snip of the scissors. They found a large mass in my abdomen, and Dr. Wise removed it. It was the size of a quart fruit jar. Luckily, it was not malignant.

Compelling Journey

Dr. Leeves continued to provide for my medical needs during the rest of my tenure in Naples. They were mostly in the form of athletic injuries, including sprained ankles, hip pointers, and a bursitis. I was not the toughest kid in town.

In 1953, I moved away and eventually found myself in the pharmaceutical industry. I called on Dr. Leeves as a sales rep once and gave him the details of my products.

Our paths crossed again in 1970, though inadvertently. I contracted viral pericarditis, which is inflammation of the heart lining. I will always feel the condition derived from my first trip to Las Vegas a few days earlier when I slept four hours out of eighty-four. I told you I was not a tough kid.

My first symptoms were chest pains, and I went to an emergency room. When I explained my symptoms, the attending physician placed me on a bed, and hooked me up to a heart monitor.

Having watched **Ben Casey** and **Dr. Kildare** on TV, I knew all about heart monitors. As long as the blip was going, you were okay. When the line went flat, your goose was cooked. Anyway, I was lying there watching the monitor, and the line went flat. For some idiotic reason, I was very calm. I looked at the monitor, and waited for my life to fade away. I waited and waited. *This sure takes a long time.* I thought.

After about five minutes, a young attendant came into the room, noticed the monitor, and proceeded to slap it rather forcefully with his hand. It immediately started blipping again.

"This crazy machine is always doing that," he said and left again. Strangely enough, I didn't faint.

Later I wrote to Don Nance, a classmate who remained in Naples, chronicling the incident about the monitor. He showed the letter to Dr. Leeves, who took it to a medical meeting and read it to the audience. The consensus was someone with such a weird sense of humor probably would not die of a heart attack. So far, that is holding true.

The incident that defined Dr. Leeves in my eyes occurred in April 25, 1982. My beloved natural cousin and foster sister, Ellie, lost her long and terrible battle with cancer. She called me to Naples earlier, and I was staying in her apartment when she passed. Someone called from the hospital when it happened. The phone was in another room, and when it rang during the wee hours of the morning, I did not hear it. Later I did hear a knock on the door. It was Dr. Leeves. He was concerned as to why I did not answer the phone, so he came by to check.

Having spent 25 years in the medical field and having known virtually thousands of physicians, I must admit to becoming jaded in my attitude toward the profession. I asked myself, how many doctors would have gone to the trouble? How many would have shown such concern for a former patient, whom he had not treated for almost 30 years? Not many. The act transcended the normal doctor/patient relationship and moved into the area of being a good neighbor.

I often wonder how many special concerns Dr. Leeves has shown other people during the more than fifty years he cared for area residents. It occurred to me that someone ought to record some of those instances, but then reality tapped me on the shoulder. There would not be enough writers or that much paper. The process would be endless. I can only say that in my mind, Dr. Leeves is an exceptional man whose contributions to the area have been so numerous and so consistent as to appear commonplace. We cannot take this man for granted. I sincerely hope other area residents will take the time to voice your appreciation for Dr. Leeves, who has meant so much to us all. I say this, knowing he will kill me, the next time he sees me.

DR. JAMES LEEVES

46

Truth is usually the best vindication against slander—Abraham Lincoln

RUNAWAY

During the years Nancy and I bounced around the country, we lived in Denver for a time. The sport of skiing had never tempted us and never would have had we not dwelled so close to the action. When one lives in Colorado, one skis.

Our first foray onto the slopes was uneventful and consisted mostly of lessons and hot toddies. The instructor ran us through the paces, and then took us to the mountain top. We made our way down. Notice that I didn't say we skied down. We made our way down, and then we chose to master the bunny slope for the rest of the day.

The next trip was a weekend jaunt to Keystone. Since we had already skied at Loveland for a couple of hours, we considered ourselves season vets. Our first instructor at Keystone went through the lessons again and proceeded to select those ready for the slopes. Strangely, he omitted our names. I was incensed by the oversight, and we decided to dispense with further instruction and use the intermediate slope on our own.

We trudged to the lift, a primitive apparatus, and mounted the seats. Getting on was easy. Getting off was another matter. When we reached our destination, I bailed out and crashed into the snow. Nancy flung herself out into space and proceeded to jam her ski pole into her ribs, momentarily interrupting her breathing apparatus. I prayed for her because I couldn't regain my feet to help in any other way.

Finally, we began to make our way down the mountain. We had to. There was no other way to get back to the lodge and remove the ski boots. I can think of no medieval torture instrument that would even come close to the pain of ski boots.

To expedite the trip down, we began our figure eights and were doing well as long as we didn't look at each other. On the few occasions when we did, we fell down laughing. I decided that I would die from old age before reaching the bottom if I waited for Nancy so I picked up the pace a bit. I am convinced that Nancy belongs in the Guinness Book of Records as the world's slowest skier, but she insists that the honor is mine.

The figure eights became smaller and smaller. Finally, I was heading down the mountain full speed waving my arms and yelling "runaway" at the top of my voice. I knew that all I had to do was fall down, but traveling at the speed of light, that did not strike me as being an option. Other skiers peered at me askance, as I flashed by. A line of skiers trudged across my destructive path and a picture filled with casts, crutches, and caskets flashed before my eyes. Those poor innocents were blissfully unaware that they were looking into the face of death. I cast my poles aside and headed between two elderly skiers. They waved as I passed.

As the parking lot loomed ahead, I viewed the seriousness of the situation. Fortunately, it was not crowded, and I was able to flash across, find a seam between a Caddy and a maroon pickup, and bury myself in a pile of snow that was a remnant from the ice age. After a moment of repose, I extricated myself, took off those instruments of Satan, and vowed never to get within a hundred yards of anything that even smells of skiing. So far, my vow is secure.

47

The free thinking of one age is the commonsense of the next—Matthew Arnold

THE FIRST LAST DINNER DANCE 1990

The spring dinner dances were opportunities for the social organizations at ET to strut their stuff. The school calendar provided a Saturday for each club to decorate the Student Union Building (SUB), invite representatives from the other groups, and dance the night away to the big band sounds of the East Texans.

To appreciate the communal harmony of the times, one must visualize the SUB, the social center of the school. The building was a relic of World War II that had once served as an activity center for service men. Somehow, the college had the structure dismantled and rebuilt on the campus of ETSTC. The main building was an open area perfect for a large dance floor, tables and chairs along the perimeter, and a bandstand. The second floor offered more tables and chairs for the ongoing card games and conversations. Attached was a coffee shop and bookstore on the west side and a game room filled with ping-pong tables on the east side. The SUB provided many hours of relaxation, since we did not live by bread alone.

During the third period, when most students were free of classes, we gathered in the SUB, had a quick soft drink or coffee, and caught up on the latest campus fare. Many of us forged relationships in this social environment that would endure for a lifetime.

The social clubs of that era gave their membership a built-in set of friends, a social structure, and activities galore including intra-mural sports, leadership training, and an ongoing opportunity to meet members of the opposite sex. Most of the clubs ceased to exist around 1960 when they chose to join national organizations. However, some members still maintain a close relationship with their club brothers and sisters through various activities.

The power of the memories from those times led to the desire to take one more journey down the social path of the forties and fifties. We remembered each other. We cared about each other. We wanted to see each other one more time, so we planned The Last Dinner Dance. Just to be on the safe side, we called it the First LAST DINNER DANCE just in case we wanted to stage a Second LAST DINNER DANCE.

Almost 500 of us gathered in Dallas in 1990. The event went so well that the committee planned and executed the Second LAST DINNER DANCE. However, the committee saw fit to call it the First LAST DINNER DANCE II, which always confused me. II was highly successful as well.

Let us give credit where credit is due. Robert Hamm and Bill Phillips did most of the grunt work for both dances, especially II. I suspect that Jace Carrington brought in more people through his months of personal contacts than any other worker on the committee. It never got any better than that.

Compelling Journey

One only has to count the number of Blue Blazer awards that originated from this event to appreciate the impact the First LAST DINNER DANCE had on alumni affairs. It is a tribute to the original committee members, subsequent committee members, and Sam McCord, the alumni director who brought in the resources of the University that this series of alumni events has endured.

48

How much easier it is to be critical than to be correct—Benjamin Disraeli

Fan Fun

As you know, dear reader, there are some things in life that have no real importance, but when one experiences them, its like scratching a fingernail on a chalk board. It's irritating.

We had this fan. It came with our house, and we had lived here seventeen years at the time, so the old fan had been around the block a few times. It made a noise when it ran, which is where the chalkboard came in, and we ran it at night year round.

I had a brainstorm. Why not put the quiet fan from my office into the bedroom, and we could buy a new fan for my office? "Go for it Big Guy," says Nancy, the resident heiress.

I go to Home Depot, buy the fan, bring it home and take it out of the box. That was the highpoint of the weekend. I spent the next two days taking down fans, moving fans, and wiring fans. The new fan worked great in my office. The former office fan worked great in the bedroom. However, young Nancy discovered a glitch. The bedroom fan had no light fixture.

"No problema," says I.

I journeyed back to HD and purchased a light kit. It was at this point that things began to turn ugly.

Compelling Journey

I attached the light fixture and turned it on. The fan starts going 90 mph. The lights became so bright that it was like looking into the sun. Then, they started blowing out.

"Aha!" Says I. "I had best turn off the lights."

A couple more trial runs result in more blown bulbs. I confessed to Nancy that I may have to return the old fan to the office and put the new fan in the bedroom. She is unsympathetic, and I figured that if I had lunch, I would need to prepare it myself.

So I put the new fan in the bedroom and, voila, bulbs start breaking and the fan went nuts. I cut it off only to discover that my bathroom lights are kaput along with the outside nightlights. I still find it strange that Nancy's bathroom lights are burning brightly. I laid my finger alongside my nose and thought...*hmmm.*

After flipping switches, turning dimmer switches, and pulling chains, I finally reach an agreement with the bedroom fan for the night, and we decide not to call the electrician until the next morning.

Don't ask how much it costs but both fans now work properly. The lights all work ... I think. There is one small glitch. This evening, the lights in the bedroom, my bathroom, and outside all went out. I flipped the breaker switch a couple of times, and they all came back on. It appears that I am not finished with the electrician, but at least I don't have to listen to that damn fan ever again.

49

A man cannot be too careful in the choice of his enemies—Oscar Wilde

SEPTEMBER 11, 2001

I clearly recall December 7, 1941. I was seven years old at the time and knew enough about the situation to feel a measure of fear. The result of the *Day that will live in Infamy* was a lingering conflict that touched the lives of everyone for the rest of their lives and snuffed out millions.

The continuing impact of September 11, 2001 is virtually crashing into our existence, just as it did the WTC, the Pentagon, and the Pennsylvania field.

The best way I can bring the reality of 9-11 into focus is to transplant the event to downtown Dallas. Imagine how it would affect the Metroplex. Imagine how many people that we know personally would now be at the bottom of that pile of death. The events of 9-11-01 forever altered my TV image of the people of Manhattan.

It is as if the foundation of our lives is a house of cards. Playing the game, we gave our savings to fledgling companies in order to reap profits unheard of in our history. We thought nothing of placing our lives in the hands of airlines to deliver us to all points on the globe. We gave up the security of lifelong benefits to enjoy a higher current income from our employer. We bought enormous houses, luxury cars, and spent large sums on our abundant leisure time. We lived the good life. Now conditions may change.

Compelling Journey

I never really thought about the consequences of a successful terrorist strike. I knew that lives would be lost but they would be someone else's life. I knew that I would be concerned, but that we would just send out a few cruise missiles and take care of the matter. Our physical or financial world wouldn't be affected all that much.

How has Osama bin Laden's brainchild affected me? My golfing vacation in Canada ended at the Dorval airport in Montreal on 9-11-01. After dealing with the shock, we tried for four days to find a way home. Nancy and I were able to fly to Toronto, rent a car, and drive out of Canada. Of course, the rental car price quadrupled. No matter that tens of thousands of travelers were at the mercy of events, the American carriers would not honor the Canadian Airlines tickets that we had already paid for. We ended up using round trip frequent flyer tickets to get back to DFW. Anyone need a couple of tickets from DFW to Detroit? Me neither.

During the days and weeks that followed, along with other investors, I watched my life savings dwindle each day as the markets tumbled. After losing for 18 months before the event, another 17% disappeared after the 11th. The selloff of large numbers of stocks by individuals triggered computer generated selloffs by the big mutual funds, and the bad situation increased exponentially. Nancy and I worked hard to secure our golden years, but it appeared that our efforts were in vain. Fortunately, the market came back along with our savings.

Air travel, one of the hubs of our economy, is under seige. The automotive industry will suffer because most buyers will choose to wait another year to purchase a new car. Many simply won't have a job to make the payments. Most people will curtail their leisure activities, and that industry will suffer. Spending will drop so the demand for goods and services will decline. Companies will have no market for their projects and no need for many of their employees. Food and shelter will become important. The sports craze that exploded over our nation for decades will decline.

I grew up in a small East Texas town that was still suffering from the Great Depression when WWII broke out in 1941. The war years bought relative prosperity to the region. Not so today. We just finished the golden age. This war will cost enormous personal sacrifice on the part of our armed forces, sacrifice on the part of you and me, and vast sums of money.

Periodically, we find ourselves in a state of war. Some are justified. Some are politician's wars designed to promote a political party and prop up a bad economy. The war in 1941 saved the economy and the nation. This one will save the country as well.

War has changed. There may not be clashes of large armies in the field. The weapons are stolen commercial airplanes, vials of bacteria, cylinders of chemicals, and the wills of the participants. This is the most patriotic USA witnessed since 1941, so the will is there, at least at present. I suspect that we will not resolve these issues quickly. We must maintain our resolve even as conditions get worse or better. We need to recognize and meet our enemies on whatever field is required.

This is truly a world war. This is a religious war. We are not only defending the Christian religion but are defending the right to practice all religions including the right to be a Muslim in this country.

I attended a Protestant church service last Sunday. It was the first time I had ever heard the Star Spangled Banner sung in church. It was a very patriotic service and everything went well until the minister referred to the

Compelling Journey

Muslim religion as being a cult. How shortsighted. How unfair. That is like assigning the Oklahoma City bombing to all white Anglo Saxon Protestants.

Yes, conditions changed. We cannot even imagine the challenge ahead. However, we are a smart people. We are problem solvers and Osama bin Laden is simply another problem, just as Adolph Hitler and General Togo were problems. I get the impression from countries around the world that all fear the sleeping giant. I hear very little rhetoric from our current enemies. It is not a good time to prod the giant. When the giant wakes up, he is grouchy.

Note: In May of 2011, a team of Navy Seals raided the home of Osama Bin Laden and killed him. The end of the war is nowhere in sight.

50

THERE IS NOTHING I LOVE AS MUCH AS A GOOD FIGHT—FRANKLIN D. ROOSEVELT

THE GREAT DOORBELL CAPER

It was about 11 p.m. As I surfed the web, the doorbell rang. I rose from my roll top desk, trudged to the front door, and turned on the outside light. I opened the door and found the door stoop empty. *Hmmm*, I thought. I peered around the front yard and saw no one. Slightly bewildered, I closed the door and resumed my place at action central.

Just as I was about to improve on Einstein's Theory of Relativity or read another email joke, I forget which, the doorbell interrupted my intense concentration. Somewhat irritated, I rose; walked back to the door with quickened pace, flipped on the porch light, and opened the walnut stained door. By this time, I was prepared to share my thoughts with the person on the other side. Alas, there was no one there.

Then, it dawned on me. My grandchildren had visited for the weekend and left for home late in the day. Because of their presence, neighborhood kids trooped in and out of our house all weekend. *It is possible*, thought I, *that some of the neighborhood kids believed that the twin girls were still at our house, and they are just being kids.* I left the outside light on just to be on the safe side and returned to the internet.

After five minutes or so, the doorbell rang. I hurried to the door, but saw no one through the peephole. Partly from irritation and partly for fun, I hid behind a drape and peeked out for about ten minutes, hoping to catch the little rascals, and scare the daylights out of them. However, no one showed, so I went back to my computer.

Not more than three minutes passed and the doorbell rang. I just sat there, and it rang again. By this time, my patience and general good nature departed. I became angry as a hornet. I visualized the doorbell ringing for the duration of the night so I decided to call the cops.

The dispatcher listened to my tale of woe and promised to send a patrol officer to the street in short order. I went back to my emails and after about fifteen minutes, my doorbell rang. I went to the door and found a patrol officer there. He was a nice young man, who sympathized with my plight. We agreed that the perpetrators were most likely kids, and he promised to hide out, catch them, and put the fear in them.

"Wonderful," I said.

By this time, it was past my bedtime, so I signed off and hit the hay. Apparently, the mystery doorbell ringer went to sleep as well, since we were not disturbed during the night.

The next day, I am reading my emails when the doorbell rings. I went to answer and found no one there. "Please, not in the middle of the day," says I. I go back to my computer, start to work, and the doorbell rings again. Then, from the far reaches of my shriveled brain, a flicker of light comes on.

Understand that this was before pop-up advertisement inhibitors. I used a cable provider, and one of the ads that popped up on a regular basis was about the price of homes in the Metroplex. When I touched the ad with my cursor, a doorbell rang. The sound came through my speakers and sounded exactly like my own doorbell.

51

Eighty percent of success is showing up.
Woody Allen

TRIP TO NAPLES
2002

Don Dawson, a classmate from the first grade through the twelfth, and I met in Mt. Vernon, Texas, about 9 a.m. and tooled on down to Nett's café in Naples, Texas, to visit a few friends. We arrived a bit early but found Don Nance and Rocky Moore enjoying a cup of coffee. The final eight turned out to be Billy Williams, Ben Grimes, John Wright, Bob Brock, Don Nance, Rocky Moore, Don Dawson, and me.

The content of our two-hour conversation was typical. We talked about nothing much and everything we could think of. Getting a word in edgewise was not always a given. Those with good manners usually never got heard. It was the same way on the playground when we grew up.

We spoke of the drought, the city of Naples, Pewitt athletics, the past and the future, and recent health reports. I still believe that I am the sickest. We rehashed the Clarksville mud game and the Atlanta championship game, both played in 1952. We still didn't win either. We spoke of Sunshine Franklin and decided that a more colorful character never lived. We remembered Donald Roberts and Forrest Babb. We always remember Forrest Babb.

Compelling Journey

The good thing about age is that we can discuss the same topics time after time but since we can't remember the last conversation, the information always sounds new. Works for me! For instance, I remembered Don Nance as the extra point kicker on our football team. Disrespectful attendees corrected me, pointing out that even though Don kicked a couple, Bobby Presley was the extra point kicker. I also recalled Don Nance as being the kickoff man, but it seems that Billy Williams performed that chore. Sometimes, I wonder if something has tampered with all of my memories, and that I don't really remember anything.

The conversation took some strange turns. You start to school with someone in 1941, spend 12 years in the same classroom, and think you know them. Wrong! In fact, I learned that I didn't even know their names. Billy Williams told the story of how the name on his birth certificate was Billie Williams (no middle name). We called him Billy Charles Williams since we have known him. In fact, he had to take legal steps, with the help of his mother, to get his certificate corrected in later life.

The same with Don Nance. We always called him Donald Louis Nance, but it turned out that the name on his birth certificate is Don Louis Nance. It doesn't really matter since most of us use more colorful names when referring to Nance.

Speaking of names, several people dropped by our table and chatted with us. One was Tiny Bub Cobb. One of the participants told a story about Tiny Bub's first day at school when the teacher asked him his name. Well! Let's not even go there.

Lois Smith was usually at Nett's, when I visit Naples, and this was no exception. This 96-year-old wonder stopped by our table and called us all by name. Even though I never really liked the woman, I wish someone would spend some time with her and record her memoirs. Lois has seen a lot of the local history and still has the mind to share it.

Naples is like a magnet. It draws me back and lets me relive a bit of personal history. However, I need my old friends there to help guide me along the way. That Saturday was a good trip, and I hope there will be a few more.

Note: Lois passed a few years ago at the age of ninety-nine. I wonder who she loved.

Don Louis Nance passed in 2012 as did Bill Bowden, another classmate. We had a wonderful reunion in July. Don just missed it. Bill couldn't make it. He had some medical tests.

Naples, Texas

52

If this is a blessing, it is certainly very well disguised—Sir Winston Churchill

Chicken Leg Coker
2001

Many of us were aware of Jack Coker's battle with cancer and knew that his time was short. That made it no less sad to lose such an old friend/enemy.

Jack and I go back a ways. While we were never close friends due to the difference in age and social status, we both grew up in Naples and spent many years in close proximity. My first association with Jack began in 1941. He was in the fourth grade and I was in the first.

My foster sister worked as a waitress at Joe's Café which was next door to Coker Chevrolet. It soon became apparent that both Jack and I went to Joe's for lunch since this were the days before school lunches. Jack soon decided that we needed to run from the school to Joe's together, eat identical lunches, then run back so we would have some play time before school began again. The lunch consisted of a hamburger, a Coke, and a double-dip ice cream cone. The total price was $.25.

Jack's grandfather on his mother's side was named Lister. Like so much of Northeast Texas, the area south of Naples was once a plantation owned by the Lister family. Jack was born into relative wealth. His dad owned the Chevrolet dealership and served on the board of regents of

Earl Stubbs

East Texas State Teachers College where Jack and I went to school.

Jack was a bright student, a teacher's favorite, and a natural leader. He was also a bully and an elitist. He usually planned the before school activities among the boys. One day he might choose a belt line. We would all line up and smack anyone foolish enough to run through the line with our belts. Should any of us fail to take our turn at running through the line, Jack or his buddy Richard Cole, would remind us.

Another activity Jack promoted was gymnastics of sorts. Three guys would bend over and lock arms. Then a fourth would get a running start and turn a flip over the others. It required some athletic ability and coordination.

My best friend was Don Dawson, a tall boy with spindly legs. Jack called him Chicken Leg. Dawson and I began calling Jack Chicken Leg and it more or less stuck. Jack's prank turned against him.

Jack was the only student at Naples High to have his own car. It was a Model A Ford in perfect condition. His ET car was a gorgeous blue 1953 Chevy convertible. It was the best car on campus.

Jack was an intense person. Sometimes that worked in his favor and sometimes not. He has a flair for the dramatic. I believe that this influenced every aspect of his life. I saw it in his athletics and his political adventures. I clearly recall some of the scenes in a high school one-act play when Jack played a priest. The judges must have liked it since he was chosen best actor in the competition.

I recall Jack as a freshman football player at Naples. He weighed about 105 pounds and played guard. If my memory serves, he became the starting guard. He was a ferocious competitor. Eventually, he developed into an all-district quarterback.

Compelling Journey

His senior year basketball team was even more impressive. With the tallest player being only 6' 4", Coach Bill Bishop took the team to the famous Dr. Pepper Tournament in Dallas. After losing a squeaker to one of the big Dallas schools, the Buffaloes went on to win the consolation trophy. This was quite an achievement for a tiny class B school.

I will always associate Jack with the FFA program, probably because he and his class initiated me and my class into the program. Jack was later to initiate me into the Tejas Club at ET using many of the same disgusting rites of passage.

Our Vocational Ag teacher was O. E. Miller. He was a prince of a man. Jack and his classmates never called him Mr. Miller. It was always just Miller. I recall that once during the summer I saw Miller, Jack, and Richard Cole running back and forth on the streets of Naples peppering each other with BB guns. I may have been one of the few witnesses to this drama of small town fun and mutual affection.

Another incident typical of Jack Coker was the FFA bus trip to the State Fair in Dallas in 1949. Don't ask me how, but Jack had a fist full of tickets for the SMU/Rice game in the Cotton Bowl that afternoon. The price was $2.75 and that put a serious dent in my $5.00 allowance for the trip. However, as it turned out, seeing Doak Walker, Johnny Champion, Kyle Rote, and his cousin Tobin play football was priceless.

When Don Nance, another Naples boy, and I went to ET in the fall of 1953, Jack and Richard were already there. The Tejas Club was rife with Naples graduates so even though I cared little for social clubs, Jack was very persuasive, and he usually got his way.

Earl Stubbs

Nance and I pledged Tejas. Jack and Richard took up where they left off in high school making our lives miserable in a fun loving way.

Since Jack was the only Naples guy with a car, Nance and I bummed rides back to Naples on occasion. Once, while riding back, Jack asked me whom I was going to invite to the next Tejas dance. I told him I had thought about asking a freshman from Plano named Pat Craig. Jack grumbled a couple of times and shared that he had planned to ask her himself. Since we were still a good distance from Naples, I did not contest the issue. They married and the rest is history.

Jack was always one of the big guys as I was growing up. He was good at most things and someone to emulate. I dreaded this day.

See you around Chicken leg.

1954 CHEVROLET

53

All dressed up, with nowhere to go—William Allen White

THE STATE CHAMPIONSHIP 2005

A Paul Pewitt High School crowd, estimated at 5,000 or more, greeted the Bulls before the beginning of play for the 2A Division II Texas State Football Championship. Our players exhibited energy and confidence, and they were ready to play. Unfortunately, the Celina Bobcats immediately regressed to gamesmanship and remained in the lockerroom.

The Pewitt squad stood around for what seemed an eternity waiting for Celina to join the event. Time continued to pass, and, finally, a few Bobcats strolled out onto the playing area. Then, while the enthusiasm of the Bulls slowly eroded, the Bobcats went through a long, time consuming ritual that I am sure was routine for their team. A few would come out, then a few more. There was a gathering, a charge, and then another gathering. The Bulls were standing, staring, and losing their edge. They were not, however, losing their talent as the game would show.

On the opening kickoff, the Bobcat kicker danced and pranced and finally put the ball in play. The first series told the story of the game. Celina installed 9 down lineman and dared Jesse to run. The chess game began as the coaches probed, attacked, and looked for a weakness in a formidable opponent. The Bulls loosened up the Celina defense by winning the battle on the line, and they advanced to the red zone where the Bobcats stiffened. The Bulls had a first down inside the 10 but could not punch it in. They settled for 3 points with a field goal.

The awesome Bobcat offense took the kickoff and put the ball in play. The first play from scrimmage resulted in a Bobcat back breaking free for big yardage only to be blindsided by a ferocious Bull tackler. The Bobcat went one way and the ball went the other. Bulls ball.

Pewitt quickly moved the ball inside the red zone once again and once again, the Bobcats raised their level of play a notch. Another field goal.

Pewitt kicked off and a Bobcat broke free and raced for the end zone. There was a blocker in front and one lone Pewitt player to save the day. What transpired was one of the best football plays I have ever seen. A blocker was between the Bull and the ball carrier. The Pewitt player showed patience, worked both opponents to the sideline, and forced them out of bounds. He saved a touchdown. Unfortunately, Celina was still able to drive the ball into the end zone, and the score was Celina 7, Bulls 6.

The highlight of the first half was a long, time consuming drive by the Bulls that resulted in a touchdown. The Bobcats appeared to be in somewhat of a daze considering how the Pewitt team dominated the proceedings. At this point, the time of possession vastly favored the Bulls, and the Bobcats appeared to slow down on both sides of the ball. The score was 12-7 at the half with momentum on the side of the Bulls.

Beginning the second half, the Bulls took up where they left off. They moved the ball and appeared to have the game in hand, but each possession, some little thing would stall the drive. There can be few mistakes against a team

Compelling Journey

like Celina. Once, Jesse broke free for what would have been a long gainer only to, inexplicably, drop the ball. He fell on it without making a first down. Several passes were to open receivers only to be out of reach. I did not feel that Teric was used enough wide to free up Jesse.

The turning point in the game was in the third quarter. The Bulls had stuffed the Bobcats at every turn and it was third and nine. The Bulls came screaming through and the Bobcat quarterback shoveled a pass to a trailing back who blasted for a first down and more. Soon after, the aggressive Bulls were caught again with a screen pass that went for over 40 yards. The Bobcats scored, went for two and made it, and Pewitt never recovered.

Pewitt struggled for the rest of the game with the Bobcat defense. Teric went back to pass. Celina rushed quickly, and he threw the ball up for grabs. A Bobcat caught it deep in Pewitt territory. They scored. Later, in the fourth quarter, the talented Celina quarterback ran for 70 yards on a quarterback sneak. No one caught him because by this time, the Bulls were fatigued.

The Celina team was tall, rangy, and very fast. They had great confidence only to lose it at several points during the game. Several were helped off the field after Bull hits. They were sure tacklers and always hit Jesse around the ankles. Their defensive line swarmed and tackled hard. Their quarterback appeared to be in excess of 6' 4" and showed his speed on more than one occasion. He passed accurately and led well. I saw no weak spots on either side of the ball, however, the Bulls were within reach of another Texas state championship until late in the game.

I have an inside source to the Celina football program. A former school superintendent there was a classmate of Nancy's, and he likes to brag. I suspect the rumors that Celina recruits prospects from other schools has some basis in fact though I have no proof. I do know that the parents of talented athletes want their children to play in Celina.

The 2005 version of the Pewitt Brahmas was the stuff of legends. Every member of the squad and coaching staff will carry positive memories of this season to their graves and well they should. Striving, competing, and winning is a rite of passage for young men. The teamwork exhibited by this version of the Paul Pewitt Brahma Bulls equals any that I have ever witnessed.

54

The only thing we have to fear is fear itself—Franklin D. Roosevelt

BIG CHANG
AND
THE PAIR OF SIXES

The cruise ship, Norwegian Dream, moved slowly through the narrow waterway that is the Kiel Canal in Northern Germany. That was the second day of a Baltic vacation cruise, the first spent crashing through the troughs of an irritated North Sea. Locals were out walking along the canal with their large dogs and small children. They eagerly waved to the passengers on the large pleasure craft as it disturbed the tranquility of the sunny morning.

Missing out on the pastoral surroundings, warm sun, and friendly Germans, I trudged up the stairs to deck ten to the ship's Casino, where the operators had scheduled a tournament of Texas Hold'em poker to take place at the ungodly hour of 10:30 a.m. The fact that I am notorious for not gambling added additional mystery to the moment. It seemed like a great idea when during the previous evening, and after a couple of glasses of wine, I signed up for the event,.

The fact that I don't enjoy gambling does not mean that I don't enjoy card games. In fact, like countless others around the world, I play Texas Hold'em almost daily on the internet but for play money, not real money. My son Mark often invites me to become involved in a real money game, but I always decline. This game was as much for Mark as for me. I plunked down the $60 and took on the bravest of the 1,700 passengers.

When I signed up, the official involved offered tips on the game if I was interested. The tips turned out to be a series of questions perpetrated by a glamorous Asian dealer on my preferences during certain playing situations. An example was, "Would you ever stay with small hole cards." My answer was an old East Texas standby, "It depends."

As the dealer questioned me, another shipboard World Champion of Poker "wannabe" hovered over my shoulder. He had already signed up for the game and was scouting out the opposition. I learned after a brief conversation that he was a high-level bridge player with numerous master points or whatever. He appeared stunned when I inquired if he had ever scored 10,000 points in one evening of party bridge. Perhaps he had never partaken of such a plebian game as party bridge.

Following through on decisions made while influenced by the grape brings to mind an old Willie Nelson song to the effect that last night I went to bed with a ten but this morning I woke up with a two. Nevertheless, I contracted for the game, so there was nothing for me to do other than avail myself of the shark pen and get the show on the road. Little did my adversaries know how much my opponents on-line feared and respected me.

There were ten players. The dealer issued $2,000 in chips to each of us and explained the rules of the game. Not everyone antes in hold'em poker. A single player antes the big blind and likewise for the small blind. Those questionable privileges travel around the table. In this game, the big blind was $200 and the small blind was $100. The amount would double every 15 minutes.

Compelling Journey

My strategy was to use the large number of players and the numerous opportunities to play conservatively in the beginning which would not be possible once the blinds were large and often. Like most plans, mine disintegrated early.

My new friend, the bridge player, sat directly to my left. I played scant attention to the other players with one exception. I noticed a large shadow covering the table and looked up into the dark sunglasses of the largest Chinese person I have ever seen up close and personal. He was 6'6" if an inch and smiled at me with shark's teeth that would make James Bond's arch enemy, Odd Job, look like a cub scout. His name was Chang. From that moment forward, I thought of him as Big Chang.

The dealer was a young, attractive Jamaican woman with a warm smile and personality to match. The pit boss lurked behind her. He exuded charm as well. Every player at the table, with the exception of me, just knew they would win the tournament and first money of $500. My goal was not to be the first one out. That almost didn't happen.

Finally, the dealer mixed the cards and dealt the first hand. I drew a king and a queen for my two hole cards. The hole cards belonged to individual players and remained hidden from their adversaries. As usual, someone felt really good about their cards and raised the pot. I covered the raise and waited for the flop. The flop amounted to the next three common cards dealt to the middle of the table. All players could use them as if they were in their hands.

I knew from countless hours of playing Texas Hold'em on line that I had a good hand. It was likely that I would get a high pair out of the flop and maybe two out of the hand.

The flop delivered another king and a queen. That meant that I had two pairs, which would lose to three of a kind and several other combinations. I didn't want to

~ 355 ~

depend on my two pairs to win the hand, so, I decided to get the shoe clerks, the undecided players, out of the hand and make a statement. Good poker players must instill fear into their opponents.

When my turn came, I went all in. I gently pushed my stack of chips into the center of the table. That meant that if other players were to compete for the pot, they must match my bet. Only the winner of the hand stayed in the game unless they started out with more money than me. Since this was the first hand, we all had the same amount of money. The risk was enormous, but I had lots of experience with pressure albeit with play money.

Texas Hold'em is a conservative form of poker where the pressure builds. Players do not like to take unnecessary chances, especially early in the game. One poor decision can take a player out of the game. If I didn't win this hand, I was gone.

Dead silence reigned. I brought my steely blues up from my cards to the next player and concentrated on the space between his eyes. He folded. The next player quickly followed. At the end, only one poor sheep chose to follow suit. He moaned when I turned over my hole cards. However, the hand was not over.

My opponent had two opportunities to win the hand. The dealer dealt the turn, a single card, to the line of cards on the table. It didn't help me or him. The final card is called the river. After a pregnant pause, he turned the card over. No help. I won the hand.

Appearing stunned, the first causality of the game reluctantly rose from his chair and vacated his spot at the table. All of a sudden, I became feared and respected. Big Chang's toothy smile lost some of its luster. From that moment on, that game was hombre contre el hombre.

Compelling Journey

During the next several hands, the play went according to expectations. I had money to burn, so I only played good hands and once lost with a full house. I won a few good pots and watched as players fell by the wayside. I noticed that Big Chang's stack matched my own and his smile had returned. He was a talented player and he knew it.

Time passed and the blinds increased to $400/$200. That changed the game somewhat. Blinds were more important but still did not justify playing a bad hand. I did a lot of folding and a little winning. During one hand, when I stayed for the turn and folded when I didn't get my card, Big Chang complained that I folded too much. That was bad form. I told him that he could tell me how to play right after he beat me. The die was cast.

The turning point came after the blind was up to $800/$400. The dealer blessed me with king/king in the hole. I played possum waiting for the flop. It produced yet another king. Mentally, I was dancing in the street. Several players bet heavily on the hand but no one had gone all in. That changed when it came my turn to bet. I pushed my rather large stack of chips to the center and three others eagerly followed suit. I figured it would take a full house to win but mine would be larger if I got it. Big Chang tossed in his cards. It was lucky for him that he did.

The turn produced at least one and maybe two full houses. I was not one of them. The river produced a king. The other players were so excided about which full house would win that they overlooked my four kings. Finally, the dealer noticed, and three players went home. That left the bridge player, Big Chang, and me.

The blind was important at this point. If one invested $800 in the big blind and called a couple of $500 bets, the flop could be hard to come by. I stayed with my game plan and drew the ire of Big Chang on more than one occasion by folding when the flop didn't produce or if I had poor cards in the beginning. He picked up on this and began to bluff on every hand. He intended to drive me out by winning early pots and it was working.

Big Chang and the bridge player went all-in and the bridge player was gone. That left just me and Big Chang. His evil smile was back, and then it occurred to me. This was the ultimate game. This was good versus evil. I represented hope and he despair. The gods were involved.

By this time, blinds was $1600/$800. I knew I couldn't continue to be conservative but would have to take wild chances. If I had even decent hole cards, I went all-in. Big Chang would fold. If he went all-in and I didn't have a strong hand, I folded. Finally, I won a couple of good hand and my stack was slightly larger than his. The playing field was level. It just came down to who got the cards.

On the last hand, I had jack/six in the hole. Big Chang didn't ever hesitate. He went all-in and, having little choice,

Compelling Journey

I followed suit. He showed ace/queen. It appeared that I was toast.

The flop was king/ten/eight. No help for me. No help for him. The turn was a six. I had a pair and Big Chang had squat. I commented, grinning from ear to ear, "Game over!" Big Chang hemorrhaged. The river was a seven. Big Chang gave off a guttural roar.

There were other Texas Hold'em games during the course of the cruise. I was dying to get in, but the fact that I could leave the ship as a winner wouldn't allow me to play. Big Chang turned out to be a high roller. He was in every game and did very well. I don't remember ever passing through the casino without him being there. He begged me every day to enter the games, but I told him I just wasn't a gambler. I was a player. Finally, he offered to back me in Vegas, but I declined.

55

You see things; and you ask "Why?" But I dream things that never were; and I say "Why Not?"—George Bernard Shaw

FUN TIMES IN ITALY
2004

As I rolled past my 70th year on August 10, 2004, Nancy and I prepared to do a bit of rocking and rolling of our own in Italy. Previously, we visited England, France, Germany, Austria, and Switzerland. Since this trip, we added Estonia, Russia, Sweden, Finland, Denmark, and Greece.

We left DFW at about 11 a.m. on August 20th, flew to Raleigh-Durham, NC and enjoyed the airport for about three hours. Then, we boarded American for a flight to Gatwick near London. We enjoyed their airport for about 7 hours. Why, you ask, didn't we take off for London and do a bit sightseeing? Have you seen the customs lines at international airports ... coming and going? At any rate, the dollar didn't stack up so well against the pound so a stale sandwich was about the best we could do.

The next leg of our flight was on Swiss Air to Venice. Swiss Air just may be the best airline in the world. We arrived in Venice some 26 hours after we took off from Dallas. Not a fun time. Did I mention that I am old? Do you understand the term aching legs? Swollen ankles? I took a Zane Grey audio tape for entertainment, but since I sat next to the engines, I couldn't hear over the noise. It was much better coming back since I was at least able to get the bad guy killed.

Compelling Journey

We zipped through customs in Venice and got on the boat to our hotel. Boat? The boat docked, and the driver told us to go up the street and our hotel would be on the left. He smiled as he pulled away.

We turned to our task and found that the nearest thing to a street was a narrow opening between two medieval buildings. There was no light at the end of the tunnel. Do you understand the term narrow? When we finally got the courage to head up the hallway, we soon met another person coming down the opposite direction. Not a problem, you say. Do you understand the term narrow? We had to stop and turn sideways to let the person past. Finally, after about a block and a half, we emerged into a busy little lane and, viola, about 40 yards to our left crouched our hotel, and a very nice one it was.

Venice is a medieval city. It was formerly a swamp, but the local population saw the bog as protection from marauding armies, so the Adriatic Sea became their ally. Imagine a city with no automobiles. Canals provide the highways to and from various parts of the city and the motor boat or gondola serves in place of taxi's. The Gondolas are cute but not very efficient. The water taxis are available and pricey. The waterbuses provide the best transportation if one knew how to use them.

The streets are narrow, crowded, and full of pickpockets. I put my wallet in my front pocket and kept a hand on it whenever possible. A money belt comes in handy. Every few blocks are a piazza or square. Some are spectacular with pigeons, mimes, musicians, churches, artwork, and countless gorgeous women from Italy, Germany, etc. The feminine style in Italy is cleavage, and most younger women are in style. (I don't make the news, I just report it.)

Venice is unique in the world due to its watery ways. The city contains many ancient churches, some over 1,000 years old. It is not a large city and most walk to do their sightseeing. We took a tour of the Morano Glass Works by boat and saw a fat man make a little horse. The city is so special that like many other places in the world such as Las Vegas, Manhattan, Washington DC, Paris, London, it will never leave one's memory banks.

Next we traveled by train to Florence, which means city of flowers. It is a medieval city as well with many churches. Most churches are also museums and contain important works of art. St. Mark is the patron saint of Florence and the winged lion represents him in statues over the city. St. Catherine is also a local saint. Her head and finger reside in Florence and the rest of her is in Rome. I saw her finger. It was very artistic.

In my view, the most important work of art in Florence and maybe the world is the statue of David. Michelangelo, age 23, created this masterpiece and it literally boggles the mind. The young genius had already made a name for himself in Rome and came to Florence to serve some patron or the other. Following the money was common during the Middle Ages as well. There was a big chunk of white marble available and several local artists tried to do something with it, but all eventually gave up. Later, in Rome, we got a grasp of Michelangelo's level of talent.

While in Florence we had a tour planned for Pisa, and its famous tower, but there was a mix-up, and the travel company substituted a tour of the Tuscany wine country where we discovered grappa. I have a talent, unknown to my friends. I have the ability to sleep standing, sitting, lying down, and at any time, at any place. Naturally, I slept all the way to the winery and missed all the olive trees. I figure that if one has seen one olive tree, one has seen them

Compelling Journey

all. However, the winery was a large, very technical operation, and we capped off the tour with wine tasting. We sampled several kinds of wine, mostly Chianti of various vintages and aging. Finally, the piece de resistance came in the form of a small glass of grappa.

Vintners produce this product from the third and final pressing of the grapes, and it is about 90% alcohol. It is very similar to white lightening. It is an after dinner drink that if drank on an empty stomach would eat off the lining. I rather liked it.

After leaving Florence, we rode the rails to Rome. We were tired and had seen a virtual plethora of art and 1,000-year-old churches. We figured Rome would be anti-climatic. Our first evening there, we toured Rome at night. All of the famous landmarks, including the Coliseum, Vatican, Forum, Circus Maximus, Trevi Fountain, the Spanish Steps, etc., were lighted and spectacular. We were in awe of the city after the first event and left the same way.

The next day we launched our hands-on enjoyment of this grand metropolis. We learned to use the subway to supplement our tours, so we made the most of our time there. A tour of Vatican City began with St. Peter's Basilica. The square before St. Pete's is just as large as I imagined. The Pope's quarters are in plain sight.

Earl Stubbs

A most impressive aspect of the Vatican is unseen. It is the museum. Hundreds of yards long, it is constantly filled with people viewing the literally billions of dollars worth of art. At the end is the Sistine Chapel, Michelangelo's masterpiece. I expected it to be a small edifice but saw that it was about 100 yards long. When Michelangelo painted the interior, he was not a painter but a sculptor and architect, yet his work, to me, put all the others to shame for beauty and skill.

In addition to painting the chapel, Michelangelo designed St. Peter's Basilica. He based his design on the Greek Cross with all arms being the same length. After his death, the holy fathers changed the design to resemble a crucifixion type cross where the central arm is longer at the bottom. Nancy and I saw many churches and cathedrals, including St. Paul's in London, Notre Dame in Paris, and St. Peter's in New York, but I view St. Pete's at the Vatican to be the most beautiful, and I credit Michelangelo's talent for that opinion.

It was interesting to note that of the 150 or so pictures I took, only one showed Leonardo Di Vinci or any of his work.

We extended our trip for an extra day so that we could catch a tour to Pompeii. We had to be in the lobby of our hotel at the ungodly hour of 7 a.m., and I made myself comfortable in a soft chair in the lobby and continued my sleep. After about an hour, Nancy called the tour company and inquired as to when we were leaving. The informed her that the tour had already left, and we were not on it. We were out the considerable fee for the trip, the expense of staying an extra day for nothing, and were at loose ends. We jumped on the Metro, headed for a gigantic park and spent the day wandering around eating Italian ice cream, taking more pictures, and enjoying ourselves.

Compelling Journey

The next morning, and I use the term loosely, we caught our water taxi at about 4:30 AM and journeyed to the airport for the flight home. We flew up to Zurich, which was only a two hour flight so I hardly had time to get a nap. We flew over the Alps both going and coming. Compared to the Rockies, they were cute. We flew from Zurich to Chicago and then to Large D. I did not kiss the ground, but I considered it. I am not a great flyer.

TREVI FOUNTAIN

56

I have nothing to offer but blood, toil, tears, and sweat—Sir Winston churchill

A Magic Night
2010

It began with a group of farmers before the turn of the twentieth century. The Stubbs family, relocated from Newton County, Georgia, to Cass County, Texas, in circa 1890-1892. They were hard working people who cleared land, planted crops, and harvested. During the growing season, there was not much time or energy for frivolity; but at other times, fishing the creeks with seines and cane poles; hunting quails, squirrels, and rabbits; and playing baseball filled their leisure hours. Yep! The young men from the richly populated rural areas of East Texas gathered after church on Sundays and played America's game. After all, it had been around for about eighty years.

My father, Marvin Stubbs, was born in 1900. He was a diminutive drop-ball pitcher in those games. Having no knowledge of how to prepare his arm for a season of throwing curve balls, he was typical of players during those days. Everyone threw the ball hard on the first day. As a result of this lack of preparation, Marvin damaged the tendons and ligaments in his elbow_and was unable to pitch_effectively for very long_. Daddy described his older brother, Walter, as being of major league quality, but I had no way of knowing if he really was. However, events

Compelling Journey

unfolding during the present time suggest that he may have possessed such talent.

Hershel Stubbs, nicknamed Huck, was a year younger than Marvin. He was Walter's son. Huck and Marvin played baseball together. It is likely that Walter was still playing at this time as well. Huck was the tallest of the Stubbs clan, and considered a top-notch baseball player. Huck had two sons. One of them named Bernice Harlan, produced a son named Rick. It was with Rick that the Stubbs gene for speed and athletic ability roared to the international scene. Rick not only had speed, but at 6'4', he had size. He specialized in the hurdles, and at his peak during the seventies, he ranked number three in the world. He still owns a hurdles record at the Texas Relays in Austin. Records also show that Rick was the fastest white hurdler in recorded track history.

Rick fathered three sons two of whom became high-level baseball players. Clint was a senior baseball player at Louisiana Tech. Drew played baseball for the University of Texas and is presently the centerfielder for the Cincinnati Reds. This story is about the last night we saw Drew play.

It occurred to my son Mark and me that it might be fun to go to Phoenix and watch the Cincinnati Reds play a few games during spring break. Grandson Aaron, who was thirteen and a baseball player, was only too willing to share an opportunity to meet his famous distant cousin and personal hero.

The Reds had called up Drew late during the last season, and he paid them back by hitting a game winning walk-off homerun in his second game.

Drew completed the season with quality play. Walter would have been proud. The fact is, we didn't know Rick very well, and we didn't know Drew at all. I had met Rick years ago at a church reunion in the community where the

Stubbs family settled. I enjoyed our conversation in Flat Creek and chose to give him a call in Atlanta, Texas, and inquire if we might meet with Drew during our visit. As it turned out, Rick and his wife, Kathryn, planned to be in Phoenix, or Goodyear where the Reds play, at the same time. He offered to arrange a photo-op for Aaron. Mark and I were about as excited to see Drew up close and personal as my grandson.

We arrived on Wednesday and went to the park, but discovered that Drew was not playing. However, Dusty Baker, the Reds manager, scheduled Drew for the Thursday night contest against the Cleveland Indians. Before the game, Rick and Kathryn arranged for a picture with Drew on the sidelines. He signed Aaron's bat and his cap. We were thrilled beyond words.

Our day was not over. Drew hit a line drive double during his first at bat, and we settled in to watch the rest of the game. After the contest concluded, Rick arranged for us to spend some quality time with Drew at a nearby hotel.

Physically, Drew is a clone of his father. He is tall, rangy, and in perfect physical condition. He lives in Austin during the off-season and works out with other professional athletes. He was gracious to us during the visit, patiently answering our questions while querying a tongue-tied Aaron about his own athletics. The best was yet to come.

Drew played again on Friday night. We had good seats behind the Reds dugout and easy visual access to the pre-game activities. The Seattle Mariners were first at bat. When their third out came, Drew assumed his position as the leadoff hitter for the Reds. He pulled a sharp single to left field, but a nice fielding play by the left fielder prevented extra bases. Unfortunately, a Reds player hit into a double play that forced Drew out at second to end the inning.

Compelling Journey

His next at bat came in the third. He casually dropped a Texas leaguer into right center for his second base hit. Again, his teammates failed to advance him to score. When Drew came up to bat in the fifth inning, the Reds had three hits and Drew had two of them. He smashed a hard line drive off the wall in right center. I figured it was worth at least a double, maybe even a triple. I began watching that young greyhound-like athlete churn around second base with unbelievable power. I also noticed that the Mariner outfielder mishandled the ball slightly. That was all that it took. Big Drew flew around third after the coach gave him the windmill. Amazingly, the Mariners managed to get the ball back in play, but after Drew hit the deck, it wasn't even close. He had just completed one of the most difficult feats in baseball-- an inside the park home run The Reds bench went wild. So did the Drew Stubbs section of Reds fans that I recruited during the course of the game.

I hope that Drew enjoys a long and productive career, but three for three with an inside the park home run is tough to beat. We were there, and, yes, I suspect is it true that great-great grandfather Walter was of major league quality.

Goodyear Arizona Baseball Park

57

This is not the end. It is not even the beginning of the end. But it is, perhaps, the end of the beginning--Winston Churchill

At my advanced age, I approach each day with the goal of squeezing the most satisfaction from it. I see darkness at the end of my life's tunnel and therein, perhaps, there is light. I refuse to accept an end to my existence. I simply cannot describe the next phase with any degree of clarity.

I hope that after analyzing this effort, my readers can see into my soul and decide that my time on this earth had some highs and lows, but that I managed even the lows with some degree of empathy.

At the end of the day, I am nothing more than an ordinary man who did the best he could with the tools fate bestowed on him. I have no special talents and no horrible flaws. I made no memorable mark while I visited this earth, either positive or negative, but I was usually able to compete. That was always important to me.

Earl Stubbs—10/11/12

Made in the USA
Charleston, SC
02 October 2013